The Eyes of Gaza

About the author

Plestia Alaqad is a Palestinian journalist and author who has emerged as a vital voice in the midst of the destruction in Gaza. At just twenty-one years old, she captivated audiences with her raw and poignant coverage of her surroundings. Through her unflinching dispatches shared on social media, Alaqad has offered the world an unfiltered glimpse into the harrowing realities of life under siege, her experiences resonating deeply with millions across the globe.

In November 2023, as the war escalated, Alaqad and her family were forced to leave Gaza. Since then, she has been awarded the Shireen Abu Akleh Memorial Scholarship for a master's in media studies at the American University of Beirut, where she continues to advocate for justice. Her advocacy has transcended borders, drawing attention to the ongoing humanitarian crisis in Palestine and calling for freedom and accountability.

Alaqad's remarkable journalism has earned her multiple prestigious accolades, including being named one of the BBC's 100 Women in 2024 and winning the One Young World Journalist of the Year Award, the Lyra McKee Award for Bravery, and a Human Rights Defender Award.

The Eyes of Gaza

A DIARY OF RESILIENCE

PLESTIA ALAQAD

MACMILLAN

First published 2025 by Macmillan
an imprint of Pan Macmillan
The Smithson, 6 Briset Street, London EC1M 5NR
EU representative: Macmillan Publishers Ireland Ltd, 1st Floor,
The Liffey Trust Centre, 117–126 Sheriff Street Upper,
Dublin 1, D01 YC43
Associated companies throughout the world
www.panmacmillan.com

ISBN 978-1-0350-7025-1 HB
ISBN 978-1-0350-7026-8 TPB

3 5 7 9 8 6 4

A CIP catalogue record for this book is available from the British Library.

Typeset in ITC Galliard Std by
Palimpsest Book Production Ltd, Falkirk, Stirlingshire
Printed and bound in India by Thomson Press India Ltd.

To Sedo, whose mint tea I grew up with; I never thought I would relive and experience your Nakba stories myself. To mama, who gave me my first purple diary and set me on my path. To my family, who never tired of reading my words and listening to my voice; now they're in a book.

And to Gaza, the soul of our souls. All that I am, and all that I will ever become. This work is for you and because of you.

Only in Gaza;
You sleep counting rockets rather than stars.
You wake up, if you wake up, to the sounds of bombs rather than birds.

Only in Gaza;
You sleep not knowing if, or how, you'll wake up.

In Gaza,
You sleep in your house,
And you wake up under the rubble.

In Gaza,
You sleep with your body parts whole,
And you wake up missing a hand or a leg.

In Gaza,
You sleep beside family and friends,
And the next day you are on your own.

Only in Gaza;
People celebrate birthdays while war echoes in the background, then welcome you into a tent with warm hands and a cup of tea.

Only in Gaza;
Despite the pain,
People remain.
Not just survivors,
But warriors.

Contents

I was only twelve years old when I began writing in my first diary.

It was a dark purple notebook with lined pages that my mom gave me as a gift – and I remember feeling excited when penning the first page, way back on 9 September 2013.

I've always believed that putting pen to paper is akin to finding a good listener, and that writing is a form of therapy. Back then, my entries often revolved around school – trivial things like a classmate not playing with me during recess, or studying hard but not getting the grades I wanted. They were filled with observations about my peers, reflections on my teachers and, of course, my crushes on boys. (In case you're curious, twelve-year-old Plestia loved One Direction. Zayn Malik was my favourite – so much so that I used to post his picture on my Facebook page to wish him a happy birthday, or congratulate him on the release of a new song. I know – cringe.) I remember falling for my younger neighbour and filling my diary with fantasies. Although I probably wasn't fully aware of it at the time, I wrote to understand myself better and to look back on the moments that had made me happy. I would love to read those diaries now, to get lost in the unassuming innocence of it all.

My first diary coincided with a tough year for me. I'd studied at the American International School in Gaza (AISG) since kindergarten, so I'd had the same classmates the whole time, and all the teachers were familiar. Everything was going well until sixth grade, when what can only be described as a friendship crisis erupted. I was getting good grades, and some of my classmates started bullying me because of it. It didn't help that my mom was the head of middle school. People accused me of only doing well because of her, and that made me sad.

Looking back, though, I believe being bullied might have been the best thing that ever happened to me, because it played a huge role in shaping the person I am today; giving me the chance to spend more time alone and develop a better relationship with myself. I learned to accept the fact that not everyone in life will like you, and that's okay. Realistically speaking, I don't like everyone in the world, and not everyone in the world will like me, and that's their problem, not mine – or maybe it's not a problem at all.

I'm grateful for the lessons I learned from a young age, but I wouldn't have survived without a powerful support system at school. Rawan Al-Sorani was one of my favourite teachers growing up. A journalist as well as a teacher, she had power and influence in our community – and she knew it. I often sought career guidance from her, and her responses only fuelled my admiration. She's the reason I decided, age twelve, that I wanted to study journalism when I grew up. When I told her that, she was incredibly supportive and started suggesting books, sparking my interest in reading and initiating my journey into writing. It's crazy to think about it now – how a decision that I took when I was twelve years old changed my life, and is the reason this book exists.

From around that time onwards, all through middle school, high school, university and life after graduation, my diary and I were pretty much inseparable.

What I didn't expect at twelve years old, when I received that first purple diary, was that future entries wouldn't contain merely trivial recollections; that they would also come to be filled with memories of living under Israeli occupation, enduring bombardments and being in a state of near-constant fear of dying, or having my loved ones be killed.

It was both insane and entirely predictable that as I grew up, I refused to change my mind about my ambitions. There was a part of me that wanted to study drama (so I could be a drama queen on stage, lol), but a louder and responsible voice in my head urged me to be practical and pursue a major that would lead to job opportunities in the Gaza Strip; ones where I could inform the world about where I lived. So, I applied to university to study new media and journalism.

Sometimes I watch Western television and I see the moral virtue seeping from privileged, safe people, who tell their kids to dream of whatever they want to be. But that's not how most of the world lives, works – survives. At least, it isn't in Gaza. For me, pursuing journalism felt like a mission more than a career.

I often think about all the children that the Israeli Occupation Forces (IOF) have killed and who they could have grown up to be. Outstanding poets and bestselling authors who never had the chance to be alive. It saddens me to think of all the potential art that will now never see the light of day. The books that will never be read, paintings we will never get to behold.

I think of Naji Al-Ali, a Palestinian political cartoonist who is best known for drawing Handala, the image of a child who is forever ten years old, and who will not grow up until he is allowed to return to his homeland. Naji created the character as a reflection of his own self – he was ten years old when his family were forcibly displaced during Al-Nakba (the ethnic cleansing and forced removal of hundreds of thousands of Palestinians in one sweep) in 1948, and Handala quickly became an iconic symbol for Palestinian people. It's crazy to me that we're in 2024, but we Palestinians can relate to Handala – who was first drawn in 1969 – more than ever before. I sometimes wonder how different Naji Al-Ali's work would have been, or would be now, if Palestine was free. We'll never know; he was assassinated in London in 1987, before I was even born.

As for me, my journey – from young idealist who dreamed of sharing the beauty of her homeland with the wider world, to hardened journalist documenting painful atrocities and losses of life at the hands of the Israeli military – started in 2019, in a cafe on the streets of Gaza, sitting among friends, the heat of the sun beating down on our skin, discussing a future that we were all too naive to realize as Gazans we had little control over.

It was hot, and I remember I was wearing a pink shirt paired with black pants, my hair worn casually, half up, half down. The cafe was called Gloria, right in the heart of Gaza City, and we had a beautiful seaside view. My friends and I had graduated high school a few weeks earlier, and we were talking about where we'd all like to go to study. Some wanted to stay in Gaza, while others were planning to go abroad to Turkey or France, or even the UK.

Suddenly, all eyes turned to me: it was my turn to share my (non-existent) plan. I mentioned that I'd been accepted to universities in a handful of different countries, but none felt like quite the right fit for me. Then a classmate suggested Cyprus, where he was planning to study, and two others quickly chimed in, expressing their interest in applying as well, followed by yet another classmate. Of course, as teenagers do when fuelled by unvarnished enthusiasm, we all made a collective life decision and applied to a university in Northern Cyprus that very night. Before long, each of us had received our acceptance letters.

When I excitedly told my mom that I was off to study in Cyprus, her expression was hilarious – half-incredulous, half-amused. She didn't take me seriously. 'This is your future,' she said, 'not just a trip with friends.' To be fair, she had a point. Throughout my senior year, I had been busy applying to top universities, hunting for scholarships and taking SATs and IELTS exams. Yet, despite all that, here I was, coming home after a casual hangout with my classmates and applying to a university in Cyprus on a whim!

Looking back, I think the spontaneity of the decision was what made it right – because, of course, I did eventually convince my mother that I was serious, and the five of us moved to Cyprus. Crazy as it was, we secured our visas, embarked on our journey and even found a cafe in Cyprus called Gloria – our home away from home.

A lot of the time we like to think that we can control our lives. We depend on sensible routines and responsible decisions and pension plans, and we sign away our individuality in exchange for a more peaceful and, seemingly, more shatterproof life. But living in Gaza – really, living in any occupation zone – teaches you pretty quickly that it is impossible to make your life truly bulletproof. Because someone can come along at any time and drop a bomb on you. So, even though you don't think about it in this way, sometimes you just make a choice and you go with it; more because a choice has to be made than because it's something that you've thought about deeply. Life has to move on.

Maybe my story makes it sound a bit like fun and games, as if it is easy to just decide to travel abroad when you're living in Gaza. But that couldn't be further from the truth. In reality, there are a thousand checks before you're granted a permit. If you want to leave from Erez, you have to get permission from Israel; from Rafah, from Egypt. And in both cases, you have to get permission from Hamas as well.

The hardest part, however, is not knowing when, or if, you'll be able to return. The borders can close at any minute, which makes it risky for a student to come back and visit when they're halfway through their studies, because they could get stuck and miss out on the rest of their degree. So, the minute I left Gaza, I knew that that was it.

It would be some time until I saw Her again.

Up until this point, my life seemed to flow naturally, from the successful completion of one stage through to the next. But three years after leaving Gaza, as I stood on the brink of graduation,

I found myself wondering: what next? Should I escape reality and delay adulthood a little longer by doing a master's degree? Or should I apply for jobs and start my career proper? Should I stay in Cyprus? Or should I go back home?

My studies abroad had shown me how little people in the outside world knew about our comparatively tiny part of Palestine. I knew I wanted to show the world the beauty of Gaza, a place often unheard of and overlooked, or dismissed as a 'conflict zone' and nothing more. I think I always knew, deep down, that this was the right path. So, I decided to pursue what I had always dreamed of: returning home to put my media and journalism degree to use. I packed up three years of my life in Cyprus and set off, determined to show the world Gaza through my eyes.

I couldn't have anticipated the version of Gaza that would be.

I went home, and the first role I took was as an editor for a local news agency. I think I lasted less than three weeks before realizing that it wasn't what I wanted to wake up and do every day. Sitting in an office for eight hours, working from behind a screen? Not for me.

Afterwards, I approached Press House Palestine – an independent, non-profit media institution, which promotes freedom of opinion and expression, and provides legal protection for journalists in the Gaza Strip – and enrolled in a three-month training programme, but still it didn't feel right. Once again, I couldn't tolerate just sitting there behind a desk, editing news behind the scenes. I tried for three months, but I knew it wasn't what I wanted to do. There was more in me, and I thought the work was slowly killing whatever hidden talents I might possess. So, eventually, I went to the director of Press House, Belal Jadallah, with an idea.

Belal Jadallah was known as the godfather of journalism in the Gaza Strip. He had served as the director of media and international relations for the Palestinian National Authority in his early twenties, then as the head of the Palestinian Independent Centre for Media Services from 2006 until 2013. His experience in the field was truly one of a kind and he had a reputation for taking people under his wing when he saw any kind of potential in them. When I started at Press House, I quickly realized that people were right about him.

Belal was an incredible guy – so open and approachable. When I recommended to him that Press House should have a social media team, he listened. I pitched all the ideas I had in mind, and he immediately looked excited. From then on, myself and a colleague, Hatem Rawagh, were given responsibility for the initiative. The results of our work were outstanding; our engagement was off the charts, with our follower count increasing sharply and multiple Instagram reels reaching a million views. I was having a lot of fun and felt like I was finally making a difference. That feeling only increased shortly after, when I took charge of the English Media Club, which involved running workshops for different groups within Press House. I had people attending them who were years and years older than me, yet they were interested, they enjoyed my teaching methods and they came for the whole five-month period.

In my free time, I used to shadow my old teacher, Rawan Al Sorani, while she was filming and interviewing people in the studio or the streets. Since I was no longer her student, she started revealing some secrets. One day, she confessed that she'd never particularly enjoyed teaching, and that her ambition was to work as a full-time journalist and reporter in the field. The international media outlets were only interested in covering news about Gaza during an Israeli Aggression, she said, making it hard to work as a journalist full time. It would seem that the eyes and ears of the world aren't interested in Palestinian life, only in Palestinian death.

That made me feel frustrated – mad, even. Why should the world only know about us when there are bombings? I wanted (and still want) the world to learn about our lives, not only our deaths. I hate that when you google 'Gaza', all you get are pictures of destruction; I think, ultimately, that's what made me leave Press House. It's not that I wasn't enjoying the work – it's that I knew there was more for me to do, to show the world my home as I knew it, and I needed more life experiences – different life experiences – to do that. So, after a few months, I took a job in HR at an agency called StepUp, just to try a new challenge.

It turns out conducting interviews is absolutely my cup of tea. I loved it. Finally, nine months post graduation, I started to feel like I was figuring my life out. I began to have a social life again, and I was tutoring a fifth grader named Leen almost every day. I did this for months, and it never felt like a job – more like I was hanging out with my little sister.

Back then, a day in my life consisted of waking up early – which I hate; I am not a morning person – then heading to work, before visiting my mom at her school. Then I'd go to tutor Leen, which was honestly fun; she would tell me stories more useful than our studies. After that, I would get home, eat and shower, then sometimes take a nap or go to Q cafe with my friends. Nights saw me drinking tea with my mom in front of the TV.

Weekends began on Thursday evenings, at a restaurant called Roots, with Dana. Since I returned from Cyprus, it had become a bit of a tradition, and just getting to our table meant half an hour of greeting everyone we knew. Fridays were cherished family days, spent enjoying breakfast or lunch together, and sometimes venturing out at night. Saturdays brought (my) comedic highlight of the week – playing tennis with my friend Yara and sister Judy. Our skills were so laughable that the tennis teacher often cancelled our lessons, convinced we were beyond help – but for us the joy was in the camaraderie and laughter of it all, not in mastering the game. You don't have to be an expert at something to enjoy it, as long as you're with the right people.

I love the version of myself I am in Gaza, far more than the version of me that was in Cyprus. Back home, I feel like I have a purpose, a sense of community. Outside of Gaza, I feel like an average person living an unremarkable life. At home, I come alive. There was only one thing missing at this time: I hadn't achieved my wish to show the world Gaza through my eyes. But I reasoned that Gaza wasn't going anywhere. I thought I had all the time in the world. Little did I know.

For now, I was an ambitious recent graduate, living as normal a life at home as possible while always under the threat of constant siege.

That is, until 7 October 2023.

7 October 2023

Day 1 | SATURDAY 7 OCTOBER

I'm still half asleep when I wake up to a flurry of messages on my phone.

Friends, group chats, the company I work at. I skim through messages, barely paying attention, with my eyes still bleary from sleep. Nothing really catches my attention. There's mention of a bombing, but that's not unusual in the Gaza Strip. And so, with little strength or motivation to stay awake, I go back to sleep.

When I wake up later that day, my phone is still blowing up with notifications. This time, I check online:

> 'Israel-Palestine escalation updates: Gaza under bombardment' — Al Jazeera

> 'People are fearful of what's to come: Gaza civilians flee waves of Israeli strikes' — *The Guardian*

> 'More than 250 bodies found at site of Israeli Supernova festival – rescuers' — BBC News

Palestinian fighters have executed a raid on Israel near the Gaza Strip, killing over a thousand people and taking a couple of hundred more hostage.

Palestine has been occupied by Israel for almost seventy-five years. Palestinians have been raided, killed and taken hostage by the IOF every month for 900 months. This is the first time the opposite has happened. I'm shocked, and I don't know what to feel. I'm conflicted. History didn't start today.

I leave my room and go to talk to my mom, but she's on the phone with the delivery guy, giving him an endless grocery list. At that moment, I understand how serious the situation is. I'm four Israeli Aggressions old, so I'm familiar with what the steps taken during an emergency situation look like. One: you start stocking your house with bread, flour and lots of groceries. Two: you open the windows a little bit so they won't break from the pressure released by bombs and airstrikes. Three: you prepare a small bag that has the passports and all the important documents and you put it near the door so if you have to evacuate, you just grab it and run. Four: you move mattresses to a part of the house that doesn't have windows and you sleep there.

It's around 11 a.m., and I look from the window towards Al-Rayaheen market across the street – it's a landmark in my neighbourhood, where everyone goes to shop, the kind of place where you can always buy on credit because the shopkeeper has known you all your life. Now, all I can see are neighbours rushing in and out with bags full of groceries, not stopping to chat to anyone. I can tell that emergency mode has been initiated in every house.

My phone rings; it's my colleague asking if he can share my number with a journalist, Mohamed Abu Safieh. I agree.

Mohamed calls me later that day and asks me to send him a minute-long video, in English, reporting on what's happening. He tells me it's a chance to work with a British television channel.

I agree and immediately sit down to write a report. I ask my sister Judy to film me on the balcony of my teta's (grandmother's) house next door. We start filming, and my teta is screaming in the background: 'Come back in the house, it's dangerous out there', but we ignore her (sorry, teta) and shoot the video regardless. I send it to Mohamed, and he tells me that the news channel wants me live on air for five minutes tomorrow morning. Without thinking twice about it, I tell him yes; I'm excited that I'll get the chance to have my voice heard as a Palestinian. It's rare that we get a platform to talk about our own home; usually, others speak on our behalf.

I text my neighbour – and lifelong friend – Dana to come over, to share the news with her. My mom makes tea for everyone (her love language, I believe). And then we all just sit together in the living room, watching the news on the TV and chatting about our feelings and expectations.

Mama tells us that she woke up to the sound of bombs and thought it was rain, so she got up to bring the laundry inside and went back to sleep. I think that's hilarious. I immediately text my friends to tell them my mom thought it was raining, and many of them reply, 'yeah, same here', which both surprizes me and doesn't at the same time. How much trauma does it take to start thinking that bombs are like rain? And how much trauma does it take to consider that funny?

While discussing today's news – which is an activity that's happening in almost every household around us – mama tells us that she fears history is repeating itself. In 1948, during the first Arab–Israeli war, Palestinians fled their homes and left their whole lives behind, with only a glimmer of hope that they would return one day. My grandparents were there, and have told me stories about Al-Nakba (the ethnic cleansing and enforced displacement of Palestinians) since I was a little child.

When I share the same stories with my grandkids, I hope it will be in the presence of a Free Palestine. The chatter about Al-Nakba brings to my mind the previous Aggression on Gaza, a few years ago.

In 2021, I was a university student studying in Northern Cyprus, and I hadn't seen my family and homeland in eighteen months. I decided to go home to Gaza, taking advantage of the fact that the world was locked down and I was studying online. As a result, I wasn't worried about missing the semester should the Rafah or Erez borders close.

I remember the one-hour drive from the border at Rafah to my house, and how the whole time I was just looking out the window at my Gaza. Squinting my eyes in the dark of a total electric blackout, I could make out the names of new restaurants and cafes that had managed to open. I remember I kept thinking about what I wanted to do the next day. I had friends that I wanted to see and new places to visit. The list of activities I had planned was overwhelming.

I woke up the next day to an Aggression on the Gaza Strip. The Israelis had attacked in response to peaceful protests by Palestinians in East Jerusalem. My reaction? I was glad I was with Gaza and that She was not alone. The comfort of being together with family and friends during such difficult times outweighed the fear and uncertainty that hung heavy in the air.

In a peculiar way, being present to witness the Aggression first-hand made it feel more bearable than enduring it from a distance.

Who would choose to stay in a dangerous area, riddled with violence and pain and aggression, over being in safety in Famagusta, far from harm? I'll tell you who – a Palestinian who wants to stay in her homeland. What we really fear isn't Israeli aggression; it's having to forcibly leave our homes one day. And personally, I've always feared losing my family members while separated from them; if we are to die, then it is better for us to die together.

My Facebook posts from the time tell that story:

> Instead of celebrating the last days of the holy month with family gatherings, Eid preparations, and prayers, we're under an insane attack. Buildings with 50+ families living in them are being bombed, and for what?? Everyone is asking everybody to stay safe and to take care, but how does one do that?? My family and friends outside of Gaza text me to check up on me, and ask if I'm living in a safe area, or if I can hear the sounds around me. All I'd like to say is that no place is safe, no sound is far away, and the bombs are literally everywhere. The house is literally shaking all the time, and it leaves me shaking. I know how hopeless and powerless you might feel at such times, but please know that at least sharing what is happening and trying to educate others around you – raising awareness – is in itself a great power. Keep us in your prayers.

A couple of hours later, I posted a picture of the key of return. It is a symbol of the Palestinian refugees' right to return to their homes, as many Palestinians kept their keys when they were forced into exile in 1948. Alongside this, I posted a picture of my friend's key to her house that the IOF had bombed, and I wrote:

> In 1948, Palestinians left their houses, their memories, and their whole lives behind them, thinking they'd come back to them in only a matter of days. And now in 2021, the same scenario is happening again. The only difference is that now we have cameras and social media to share and post about what's happening. The second picture is the key to my friend's house that no longer exists. We, Palestinians, all have keys to houses that no longer exist. Yet the hope of us returning back to our homeland, Palestine, of having all our land back, never fades away!!

A few days after that:

> Last night was one of the worst nights in my life. Buildings and houses and the people inside and alongside them were demolished, and the streets leading to hospitals were bombed. Israelis have no goals and no targets left; they're literally bombing randomly, everywhere. And no, it doesn't get any better, and the tear of airplanes and sweeping of bombs have become the soundtrack of our lives, and we're feeling stressed and anxious and we're just waiting, waiting, waiting. For what? For our turns? In such times, it's a fantasy to make it out alive.

Little did I know what was to come.

You know what always inspires me? The spirit of Palestinians. How after every loss, you only find us stronger and trying even harder to live and love life. In 2021, I thought I was experiencing the worst days of my life. Buildings and houses were being bombed by the IOF; even the streets were being bombed, making it harder for paramedics to reach injured people. Yet, once the Aggression was over, there was a community initiative to clean the streets of Gaza. I immediately took up a broom and joined in. Only a few weeks later, Gaza's streets were full with Palestinians striving to live despite the harsh reality that surrounded us.

As Mahmoud Darwish, maybe the most famous Palestinian poet in history, said: 'We love life if we find a way to it.'

I remember going out with my friends to the Bellini cafe and restaurant inside Capital Mall.* We were sitting at our favourite table, by the window. To my left, my friends were eating delicious food, music and the voices of people were in the background, and Bellini was crowded with Palestinians determined to live. To my right, outside the window, I could see a demolished building that had housed several warm apartments and shops. And you know what was in front of that demolished building? Business owners who had lost their stores, selling whatever they could save from under the rubble.

You might perceive Gaza as a desperate place. And yes, there is death and there is destruction, and it's not fair and we know that there's a better world out there. But that's not what I see when I look at Her. I see only the unity and resilience of Her people. While many have been displaced and lost their lives, we

---

* Bellini is an important place in my life; my favourite waiter, Ali, worked there for many years, and he was universally loved by all his customers.

remain determined to live on, and we refuse to let the losses we've suffered dictate our future.

In Gaza, you'll find mothers of martyrs celebrating the sacrifice of their children. Does this mean that they're pleased that Israel killed their children? No. But are they proud that their children gave their lives for Palestine? Yes. It's an act of giving meaning to the worst loss a person can possibly endure. We don't celebrate death – but death is all around us, and we need a way to convert it back into life. Those parents didn't choose this. Their kids aren't soldiers who chose to die. They're kids. So, when a kid is murdered by the occupation, sometimes the only way to make sense of that loss is as part of the price tag on Palestinian freedom, and freedom from the entity that's doing all the actual killing in the first place.

My family continue to speak anxiously, but eventually, the conversation dies down, and there's nothing to do but sleep. To wrap up the day, we complete steps one, two and three of emergency preparedness, but not four. We're too lazy to bring our mattresses to the living room and sleep there, so we all just sleep in our own rooms – but we make sure the windows are open.

The Forty-Five Days

Day 2 | SUNDAY 8 OCTOBER

With tears in my eyes,
I tell the teacher,
'Israhell stole my pencil case.'

The teacher asks Israhell,
'Did you steal her pencil case?'

Israhell nods confidently,
'She agreed to give me a pencil.
So why not take the pencil case too?'

The teacher stares at me,
And says nothing,
And turns her back to the board.

I, angrily, hit Israhell.
The teacher stares at me again,
Then proceeds to admonish me.
'Go to the principal's office!'

What does the principal do?
He condemns my actions,
Turning a blind eye to Israhell.

I remain,
Sitting in the corner of the office,
Without my pencil case.

You know when you were a little kid and you couldn't sleep because of how excited you were, as if you were going on a trip the next day? That was me last night. I had a hard time sleeping, but not because of the bombs or the unmanned vehicle drones. I've somehow normalized these events; they're the only normal I know, and this is the environment I was born in. There's nothing new there. But the thought of being live on the news? Even amidst the chaos, that's new and exciting to me.

I wake up early, around 7 a.m.

Both the electricity and internet are cut off. Mohamed comes to pick me up. I don't know a lot about him, but I am expecting an energetic journalist with curly hair (we already have a lot in common). The streets are empty, which is unusual. Even though Mohamed only contacted me for the first time yesterday, the chaos has united us, and he feels like an old friend already. There's almost no one walking on the streets, and barely any cars. All I can hear is the sound of unmanned vehicle drones, a noise familiar only to the people of Gaza. To explain it, imagine a fly buzzing close to your ear. The drone does the same thing: it keeps buzzing all day, like a fly, only worse. Ten times worse

After a seven-minute drive, we reach Press House Palestine, and I conduct two interviews: one live, and the other pre-filmed, with Mohamed interviewing me. The Press House feels like a beehive, bustling with journalists who are coming to use the internet or to charge their phones and equipment. I don't know most of them. Then I run into Hatem Rawagh, my ex-colleague who works there writing the news, and editing articles, films and other content – much like he did when we worked together. Hatem is an ambitious journalist who is always willing to go above and beyond to get any job done. If you need help with anything, you just know that Hatem is your guy. I barely have a chance to talk to him – I have to leave quickly due to the danger – but it's nice to see a familiar face on the ground.

As soon as I finish the two interviews, Mohamed drives me home, because I know mama will probably be worried. And if truth be told, although it's only a seven-minute drive, I'm terrified myself. I was excited to be given the opportunity to do the interview, but it is only a temporary distraction. Gaza is already unrecognizable and it's only day two. The Ministry of Health has announced that 413 Palestinians have been killed, seventy-eight of them children, and 2,300 people have been injured – and the word 'injured' here doesn't mean bruises, sprains or strains. No. It means amputations, or severe burns.

The journey feels like it takes hours, not minutes. But now, sitting silently in the car, the gravity of the destruction and the impending danger begins to weigh on me. Yesterday, I was at home, following along with the news. Today, I'm outside, seeing the streets of Gaza around me in person. It's different – at least ten times worse than it looks on television.

I go back home and mama is awake, waiting for me. She asks me how my interviews went, and how the situation is outside. I tell her that the streets were empty but, other than that, everything seemed okay. I intentionally decide not to mention the destruction to my mom as I don't want to add more to her worries.

The intermittent internet and electricity add to the atmosphere of uncertainty, with the only way of following the news being through teta's radio, which is such a frustrating experience. The radio is broken, but it also somehow works, and teta has it turned on constantly – even while we're sleeping. It's horribly sporadic. When you need information, it is silent. When you don't, it jolts you awake.

Luckily, I have phone service, so I start texting and calling my friends for updates. A friend of mine from school sends me a screenshot of what the IOF have sent him. It's a message to the residents of Beit Hanoun to evacuate. I feel so bad for him, especially because his house had already been bombed during a previous Aggression. He used to always talk about that in school. I don't remember ever seeing him cry over his house or any of his stuff – in fact, he was always talking about how his father said that he'd build them a bigger and nicer house one day. But sometimes you could see the sadness in his eyes.

I don't want him and his family to go through it again. How many times is a person supposed to start from zero just because they're Palestinian, living in Gaza? And how many houses can a Palestinian build and work on and turn into a home, only to have an Israeli decide to bomb it? Just because they can.

Yay! Finally, there is electricity and internet again. Dana comes over, and we all gather in the living room with nothing to do except keep following the news. I am shocked by how quickly the situation is escalating, and I begin to believe that we might be facing an especially bad Aggression. Mama has thought that since the beginning, but not me, the forever optimist. Al Jazeera posts:

> Israeli air attacks and shelling aimed at houses and apartment buildings have displaced some 123,538 Palestinians in Gaza, according to the UN humanitarian relief agency.

I feel grateful that I'm not one of them, yet.

It's funny how rituals can develop in the midst of trauma. During an Aggression, there's never anything to do other than worry, so one tradition that's developed is playing cards with neighbours. Anything to distract us from the news. And you notice the smallest things. Tonight, Dana's older sister Rafaa isn't with us. She has gotten married and moved to the UAE. I am happy for her and everything, but I also miss her and, crucially, without her we don't have enough players for cards. But we adapt! Dana and I just play online with two other friends. It's hard to distract ourselves, but we try.

Later, Mohamed calls and tells me that I'm going to be live on air again tomorrow, to reflect on the latest updates. This time, I'm not so excited to be on the news, but I feel it's my duty to share with the world the reality on the ground.

It has become obvious that step four of our safety plan is necessary. Dana and I get mattresses for everyone and we sleep in the living room, because it's considered the safest area in the house – it only has one window. Dana stays; we feel safer when we're together, and I think she's afraid to sleep in her room without Rafaa, even though she doesn't tell me that out loud.

Dana and I have been there for each other during every Israeli Aggression on Gaza.

Friendships in Palestine have classifications of their own. Everywhere else, friends are supposed to be there for each other during ups and downs. But in Palestine, that includes times of violent warfare and destruction. It's insane how, living in Gaza, you know your real friends according to the Aggression gauge. Will my friends be there for me when my house gets bombed? Or when I get displaced?

You get my point.

Day 3 | MONDAY 9 OCTOBER

I wake up to internet and electricity, so I do the live interview from my house. It's unbelievable how it's only day three, yet enough houses and buildings have been demolished that over 100,000 Palestinians in Gaza are displaced. I don't want to imagine how much worse it could get.

I decide to take a nap so that time might pass faster. I've barely closed my eyes when Dana calls me, telling me that she and her family are evacuating and are going to her sister Rose's house in the Rimal area. I start panicking and go to the living room to tell mama.

After going to the front door to see what's happening – why are some people evacuating and others staying? – we learn that the IOF have sent out a warning, telling us that they're about to bomb a university close to where we live.

My family and I decide we won't be evacuating for several reasons. One, there are neighbours still in the building. Two, we don't know where to go and where else might be safe. Three, we're afraid that the bombing might start at any minute and that it's already not safe for us to move. Four, this isn't the first time a building close to us has been bombed. Five, it's hard for us to evacuate with teta because she's in a wheelchair and the electricity has cut out. Six – most importantly – the Israelis haven't contacted us directly and warned us to evacuate.

Some neighbours are panicking, closing their doors and evacuating, while others are opening their doors, mindful that it's dangerous to keep them closed. When you're under heavy fire, a door might get blown off any second, so keeping it open is safer. The worst-case scenario is your house getting burned down from the bombings, with you stuck inside and the door not opening.

We're all just waiting for the IOF to bomb the university. My family are sitting in a small corridor inside teta's house, because there are no windows there and it's supposedly safe. My neighbours have taken their windows out so they don't break. We keep moving between teta's corridor and our neighbour's house.

Eventually, the bombing starts. It's extreme enough that my family decide it's safer to go to our neighbour's flat instead. We've been living in the same building since I was three or four years old, so we have a close relationship with all the other neighbours. Now, we are ten people gathered all together in a tiny kitchen, just waiting for the bombing to stop, but it only gets more extreme, and closer.

Speaking of kitchens, mama had been cooking rice and chicken before the bombing started, and she didn't get to finish. Now, because our neighbours have rescued us, we eat lunch with them. I think to myself that it's my lucky day, because we have one of my favourite dishes: creamy chicken corn sandwiches.

And I don't even have to help clean the dishes, because no one does them. We all just eat, sitting on the floor in an area far from the windows. The dishes are staring at us, and we're just staring right back at them. I mean, we might get killed any minute, so who cares about the dishes? It starts to get dark, and the bombing stops for a while, then resumes.

I'm familiar with the sound of bombs, and there's no way it was only the university being bombed. The electricity and internet go out, of course, and we don't have any service to call anyone or to follow the news. I'm sitting in silence, which is unusual, just staring at everyone's eyes. The fear in them is louder than any words. All I want is for the night to pass, and to see the light.

I don't want to die in my neighbour's kitchen.

I feel like we are all going to die. My neighbours are all running out of the building. Nobody knows where to go. It's dark, and we can hear the bombing still going on around us, like a sick musical soundtrack on repeat. There aren't any words that can do this experience justice, but I vlog a couple of videos to try to capture it. I'll never forget the scene as my family and neighbours leave the building in shock. An apartment on the third floor – one floor beneath us – has been bombed, causing another apartment to catch fire. All that happened while we were inside the building, and we didn't know! Think about how loud the sound of bombs must be.

The Palestinian Civil Defence are taking all elderly people to Al-Quds Hospital, including teta. I insist on staying with them, and I sit in the back of their car so I don't get separated from her. My sister Judy comes with me while mama walks to the hospital with the neighbours. My dad is thankfully working abroad. Along with my older brother Ahmed, who's studying in Canada right now, he's missing out on the action. I wonder how their FOMO is doing.

When we arrive at the hospital, almost all the faces are familiar. I see neighbours who live in the same building as me, and others who live in the same neighbourhood. I'm used to seeing them in the market or at a pharmacy, not displaced in a hospital.

Teta, Judy and I arrive first and we wait for my mom and our neighbours to arrive. The sound of bombs is non-stop, and I'm scared that something bad is going to happen to them while they walk to the hospital. Luckily, they all make it here alive.

I walk around the hospital, and the more I walk around, the more familiar people I meet. It is heartbreaking. And what I see in the hospital, and all the stories I hear, feel like they need a whole diary of their own. Now, I'm writing about it and it feels like a scene from a horror movie. I wish it was a movie scene, not my life.

After a time, a young boy named Motaz comes towards me and introduces himself. It turns out he was a student at AISG too, and he recognizes me from my visits to mama at work. He and his family live in my neighbourhood and, having had nowhere to go after they were forced to evacuate their house, they came to the hospital. We sit on the stairs together, and Motaz talks to me for an hour about his best friend from school who has been injured in an airstrike. He is in the same hospital as us, getting treatment at that very moment.

Motaz is physically sitting with me, but his mind is with his best friend. He keeps trying to check up on him, but the doctors won't allow it. I stay on the stairs while Motaz comes and goes, trying to process everything that has happened over the previous twenty-four hours. Eventually, he comes back from one of his attempts and tells me that his best friend has just died.

He sits back next to me and I just listen to him. He talks about all his memories of his friend, and how he can't imagine going back to school without him. I don't believe there's anything you can say to a person who has lost someone to make them feel better, so I just offer my ears. Personally, I can't imagine losing Dana or Yara – or anyone who's a part of my life, really. If the man who works in the supermarket under my building was killed, I'd be heartbroken.

We weren't able to take much when we evacuated our home. The only thing I took with me was a small notebook with the different duas (prayers to God asking for help, forgiveness and mercy) listed. My family and I recited these duas as a tribute to my grandfather when he passed away the previous January. But at this moment, I feel like Motaz needs it more than me, so I give the notebook to him and tell him that the best thing he can do is pray for his friend. He leaves to see his family soon after that, and I stay sitting on the staircase trying, yet again, to make sense of the fact that this is all real.

Never did I imagine that I'd find myself in a situation where I'd be sitting with a fifteen-year-old stranger, comforting him over the death of his best friend. I know that might sound a bit weird: why can't you imagine yourself in that situation when you've been surrounded by Israeli Aggressions in Gaza your whole life? My answer is simple: no matter how familiar you are with something, no matter how much you think you've gone through it before and you know how to deal with it, when it happens, it hits you differently.

The hospital is getting really chaotic. It's full of injured people, of displaced people who have come here with bags that have their whole lives stuffed into them. The floors are dirty, smeared with blood and marked with people's footprints. I want to clean the floor so badly, but I mind my business. I look at the people around me and try to read their faces. It isn't hard. They're heartbroken, and scared, and tired, and sleepless.

My family and some of my neighbours find a corner somewhere with a sofa. After locating a spare mattress, we take turns sleeping in rotation, because there isn't enough space for everyone. I don't know how I'm able to sleep; the last thing I remember is having access to the internet and scrolling through my phone.

What if the Civil Defence came ten minutes late to evacuate us out of our neighbourhood? We could've been dead.

Day 4 | TUESDAY 10 OCTOBER

I don't know where to begin. Yesterday was the worst day of my life, but it seems that, from today, things are only going to get worse still.

I wake up alongside my family and my neighbours, astounded that I just had a sleepover in a hospital. We wash our faces, and my neighbour goes to search for an open restaurant – anywhere that we can eat, so we can function properly and decide what to do next. There are still restaurants open, particularly those close to hospitals, and he's able to find some falafel and several sandwiches.

After breakfast, we start discussing our options. We want to leave the hospital, to give others evacuating the chance to stay here if what happened to us yesterday happens to them. Fortunately, we still have friends and relatives with intact homes; one, Amal, invites us to stay with her and her mother. Splitting from our neighbours, who go to stay with other friends, my family and I accept.

But first, another Gazan tradition.

In Gaza, whenever someone's house or building gets bombed, the next day neighbours will gather to go check on it, hoping to salvage anything from under the rubble.

We arrive at my building. I'm shocked, both at how damaged the structure seems to be and at the fact that it looks to be still standing. We take the stairs, which are riddled with dirt and broken glass. The closer we get to the fourth floor, the faster my heart beats and the more anxious I feel. I no longer want to see the physical destruction; there's something about seeing your own possessions, your own house destroyed, that makes everything more painful.

I'm given a small reprieve; our apartment is still there. Last night, when I saw it on fire, I thought the whole floor would burn, and probably the whole building. The firefighters did an amazing job. Mama, Judy and I quickly grab one change of clothes each, and I take my laptop and all my chargers. For a second, I ask myself if there's a way that I can fit my entire house into a bag and take it with me – but then I think that we're all going to get killed at some point, so what I take from my house won't really matter in the long run.

I see that Dana's house is wide open, so I go inside and I call her to take her on a virtual tour of her home. Her mom's and brother's rooms are completely burned out, almost unrecognizable, while her room is full of debris and broken glass. But it's still her home, just like my building is still my building. In Gaza, even if your house is destroyed and the ceilings have fallen to the floor, it is still your house, and you're going to claim it as your house. Even if it's not safe, even if it's ground down to rubble, you will put a tent down on the flattened remains and you will call it your home. The connection between a Palestinian and their house is a sacred one, and nobody can or will break it.

Dana's older brother Wesam arrives to conduct his own ritual. I quickly ask Dana if she wants me to grab anything for her, and she tells me to give her brother her favourite perfumes. I mention to her that there might be more important things for her to have in the midst of an Aggression, but she insists only on the perfumes. I love that girl for so many reasons, and this is one of them.

We can't find any taxis, so we walk back to the hospital. It's only a twenty-minute walk but it feels like hours. I start vlogging, comparing our situation to Al-Nakba; I wasn't there, obviously, but I am swiftly realizing that my whole life is now in a bag that will keep moving with me wherever I go. I have no base. I am re-living the stories of Al-Nakba.

We reach the hospital. My teta joins us and we say goodbye to our neighbours. I offer a fleeting thanks to the staff there, but what can you say to emergency workers who are in a state of constant emergency? I know they're doing their best.

Before I leave, I meet Ameer Abu Aisha, who serves as both the media coordinator and the emergency operations room coordinator at the Palestine Red Crescent Society. He pretty much lives in the hospital at this point. He tells me that he follows me on social media, and that he thinks I'm a brave person. The recognition feels nice – a compliment is a compliment, regardless of when it's given. We exchange numbers in case of emergency, I thank him and then I leave the hospital to head to Amal's house.

On the way, I stop at Press House Palestine and grab a press vest and helmet from Hatem. I've decided to start working on the ground and I need to be as safe as possible. The gear is heavy. When we arrive at Amal's house, mama immediately takes a shower and I set about charging all my devices and checking my notifications, grateful to be somewhere with electricity.

We are at the house less than thirty minutes when we're forced to evacuate again; the IOF have called the building's guard and told him to spread the word that an attack is imminent. The IOF have different ways of sending warnings out. If they want to attack a specific building, they'll simply call that building's caretaker – if you don't hear from him, you don't get the message. Similarly, if they're targeting a house, they'll only warn one resident, and trust that the communication will spread. They only distribute evacuation leaflets or make a publicly recorded call when it's a whole area they're about to bomb. And sometimes? They don't send a warning at all.

There is no certainty.

The worst warnings are those that come through word of mouth. All of a sudden, everyone is panicking, people are confused and yelling, and you have no idea what's happening. Is this a rumour? Do we really have to evacuate? Will the whole building be bombed, or is it only a couple of apartments? Or maybe it's just the building across the street? Who sent the warning? Millions of questions, and countless emotions, and barely any time to process anything. You just have to move.

The quickest showers of my life have been those that I've taken during Aggressions. I've always been terrified of having to evacuate the house mid-shower. Or worse – what if the house were bombed while I was still in the shower? There's so little you can control during an evacuation; maybe it's natural to think of – and care about – how your body might be found should the worst happen.

There are six of us – all of us women and two of us elderly (teta and Amal's mom) – and a cat, scrambling to evacuate the building while grabbing whatever belongings we can. With no time to spare, I throw on my press vest and helmet, grab my phone and charger, and then hesitate when I see my laptop and my emergency bag. They're too heavy to carry – I'm already struggling with the press gear, combined with the weight of the crisis we're in, which feels like a ton of bricks laying across my shoulders.

I find myself in a situation where I have to choose between my entire life, in the emergency bag, and being a reporter. I decide that journalism means more to me than the bag that has my life and home in it, so I just leave it behind. It leaves me questioning: how many feelings can you process all at once?

We find ourselves standing in the street, clueless about what to do or where to go. Do we head back to the hospital and surprise them by returning with two extra friends and a frightened feline? Do we try Amal's sister, Rasha? She's my mom's best friend, but her house is in Al-Zahra, almost twenty minutes away by car. Gaza is so small, nearly everything is 'almost twenty minutes away by car'. And yet twenty minutes is a journey full of danger, from which we might not return. There are too many questions and we don't have time to think. It feels like the end of the world. By some miracle, we find a taxi. All five of my family get in and there's no space for me, but it's okay – because destiny (Mohamed) is calling me, asking if I can come in for an interview. He promises to drive me to my family once we're done, so I leave my family behind, telling my mom she shouldn't worry about me. I start the walk to Press House Palestine.

I'm still wearing the press vest and the helmet, so people keep stopping me to ask for the news. I'm a journalist; I'm supposed to know what's happening. But right now, in Gaza, there isn't much of a difference between journalists and civilians. Nobody has internet access, or fuel for their cars, or any reliable source of up-to-date information.

I arrive at Press House and meet Hatem at the door; he's just standing there, staring out at people in the street. The IOF has bombed Etisalat, one of the biggest telecommunications companies in Palestine, and there's no internet or phone service. People are just standing around looking a bit lost. The scene is completely bizarre.

Soon after I arrive, two of Mohamed's colleagues – Ibrahim and Mohamed 2 (nearly everyone in Gaza is called Mohamed) – tell me that he's been pulled away for last-minute work, and that they'll be interviewing me instead. We go in their press car to my neighbourhood and they film me talking about my area being bombed. I tell them I can no longer recognize my own street.

We finish the interview, and Ibrahim and Mohamed 2 ask me where I'd like to be dropped off. In reply, I ask them where they're going, and they tell me that they know of another journalist's house that still has internet, so I insist on going with them.

It turns out some parts of Gaza haven't been directly bombed and still have internet access. Press House is cut off, and Rasha's house in Al-Zahra received sporadic cell connection even in 'peacetime', so the idea of going there sounds like hell to me. I realized I'd rather die working in the field than being isolated in a house with no internet or cell coverage. I know. Priorities.

I never learn the name of the journalist who welcomes me into his home (it's probably Mohamed). I wouldn't normally go into a stranger's house and demand to use their internet, even during an Aggression, but this is starting to look like no Aggression I've ever seen before. Everyone who still has a standing house welcomes other people, even those they don't know. That's the Palestinian norm. It's survival through camaraderie, generosity and mutual support.

The journalist's house is in North Gaza. It has two floors, one for women and girls and the other for men and boys. I go to introduce myself to the women, telling them that I'm just there to use the internet for a while, and that I'll be leaving with my colleagues shortly. They're amazing and welcoming, continually asking me if I'd like to eat or drink, but I say thank you and politely decline. I won't take their food; the Aggression is just ramping up, and I know how prices in the markets will increase as supplies become scarcer, and I'm embarrassed enough to be mooching off their internet already.

They still give me snacks and a small bottle of water.

The journalist's wife is so proud of me being a journalist, and she keeps asking about her husband and what he's like in the field. I praise him and say that he's a one-of-a-kind journalist, even though I don't know him.

My time on the internet is limited, and I'm a bit overwhelmed. What's the wisest way to use it? First, I reply to messages from friends and family, to assure them I'm okay. Then, I check my Instagram, and I'm shocked by the number of followers I've gained and the amount of support that's coming my way. A vlog I recorded yesterday, at my neighbour's house, features the sound of a bombing in the background. My live reaction to that – mouth wide open in shock and fear – has gone viral.

I'm finally able to talk to Dana. She tells me that she's in Khan Younis, in South Gaza, having evacuated with her family to her other sister's house. The process of evacuation and displacement in Gaza is endless. You evacuate your house, you go to a relative's house, then you and your relatives evacuate to another relative or friend's house until you all end up in a tent together.

We leave the journalist's house before it gets dark outside. Ibrahim and Mohamed 2 ask me again where they should drop me off. I tell them to take me with them, wherever they're going, and they look at me like there's something wrong with me for not wanting to leave them. But they don't have the time, energy or capacity to argue, so I go along with them.

We reach an office in northern Gaza, only around ten minutes from my house. It still has an internet connection, so I settle in to do some more work. I conduct two more interviews with different news channels; I don't know when I'll have internet again, and I want my voice to be heard. Two days ago, I was thrilled to be live on air, and now I don't feel much of anything except numb, and maybe a little overwhelmed.

The office is just a normal building – a business, where people are supposed to be working – but it looks like a refugee camp. There are two families sheltered there, and the scene is like something out of a movie. Two women around my age, casually walk around in their pyjamas. A man, perhaps in his fifties, smokes shisha while tapping on his laptop. There is a man praying – he might have been the brother of the two girls. It is chaos; I wish I could film it. It might sound mean to say, but I'm grateful that there are no children around to cry or scream.

I try minding my own business. I'm just here to use the internet. But someone's mom comes to the office to check in with one of the others, and she gives us sandwiches and water, and I thank her and eat half of the sandwich before setting it down. I'm starving, but I feel like I don't have time to eat, and it's a tiring process to hold the sandwich, bite into it *and* consume it.

Later, Ibrahim and Mohamed 2 get a phone call, and they're told they have to go report on a massacre at Sheikh Radwan. They put on their press gear and tell me to stay in the office. I, of course, refuse. I insist that I'm going with them. They tell me that it's not a field trip, that it's dangerous and that anything that happens to me will be my responsibility. I barely listen to a word they say.

We're about halfway to Sheikh Radwan when we have to stop. The bombing there is still ongoing – non-stop – and it's too dangerous to report from there.

For the third time today, Ibrahim and Mohamed 2 ask me where they should drop me off. This time, they tell me that they're just going home – work is over for the day. After I make triple sure that I won't be missing out on covering any massacres, I ask them to drop me back at Al-Quds. I call Ameer on the way and he tells me I can use his office as a quiet place to get some work done, and the amount of gratitude I feel towards him is disproportionate to his offer.

I call my mom, to tell her I'm okay and that I'll be staying at the hospital tonight. It takes ten attempts to get through to her. When I finally do, I speak to her as though we're living in la-la land and everything is okay, and I act as if I don't fully understand why she's so worried. *What Aggression? What are you talking about?* And I think, to a certain extent, she believes me. Maybe it's an easier narrative for her to process.

My mom knows that she has little choice but to let me be myself. I'm a responsible woman who can make the right decisions when I need to, but I'm also the most stubborn person alive when it comes to wanting to do stuff. Mama knows if she tried to tell me not to work, I would routinely ignore her. There are circumstances where, as a journalist, I just can't not work. And she knows that. So, it's easier for her to trust me.

At around 6.30 p.m., I decide I'm not going to sleep at the hospital tonight. I need to shower and eat real food. I call my best friend, Yara, and tell her I'm on my way to her house. Everything in Gaza is within walking distance, but I'm absolutely exhausted. I realize with dread that, if I'm not mistaken, I've left my wallet in mama's bag, and I don't have any money at all. So I do something embarrassing, and ask a taxi driver if he can drive me to Yara's for free. He agrees on one condition: 'When I get killed,' he says, 'post a nice picture of me online, and ask people to pray for me.'

Everyone in Gaza knows that they'll eventually die, and that it's only a matter of time. I smile at the taxi driver and assent.

I can't tell you how relieved I am when I get to Yara's house. I've known her since we were both in the fourth grade, and I've spent as much time at her home as I have my own. The first thing I do is take a shower; she gives me a fresh pair of pyjamas to wear (the top and pants don't match, but it's *fine*, I guess). Then her dad bakes *manakeesh* (a thyme-and-oil-topped flatbread), and I think it's the most delicious thing I've ever eaten in my life.

It's a small reprieve before the inquisition starts. There are over twenty people in the house at this point – Yara, her mom, her dad, her brother and his wife, her uncle and his family, her family friend and her kids, and her brother-in-law and his family – and everyone starts peppering me with questions about what's happening outside, and what it's like to be a journalist in such circumstances.

It was a very long day today, so to say I'm tired is an understatement. The minute I close my eyes, I'm asleep.

I wake up in the middle of the night, and stare over at Yara for a bit, thinking, *Wow, this is actually happening.* I wonder if she realizes that this is our first-ever sleepover.

At this point, I'm just writing, though I don't really understand a word. Sometimes we act delusional to protect ourselves, I guess. But I don't know if I'm writing about my real life, my real experiences, or if it's just a script for some movie. I just keep writing. And I keep processing. And I desperately hope that it works.

Day 5 | WEDNESDAY 11 OCTOBER

Yara and I wake up early. She makes tea for us both, and we sit on the stairs of her house, drinking it. I've barely taken a sip before Mohamed calls me, telling me to get to work.

I wander the streets and I don't recognize most of the areas I pass, even though these are avenues and roads I use on a daily basis. The destruction has rendered them unidentifiable.

Mohamed and I go to report on Al-Krama district, which was bombed yesterday. My heart breaks when I see family photographs randomly scattered under the rubble, and I feel terror thinking of the day when Israel will kill me, and random people will walk in the street, see my diaries discarded under debris, and wonder who Plestia Alaqad was and why she died when she did. I'm finding it difficult to absorb how fast the situation is escalating, and how terribly.

The toughest part of the day is when I visit the UNRWA school, and see the families and children staying there. I'm trying to find words to describe how horrible the scenes are, but I can't. According to the UN Office for the Coordination of Humanitarian Affairs (OCHA), by day five there are 338,934 displaced people in Gaza, of whom two-thirds are sheltered in UNRWA schools. The number of displaced has increased 30 per cent over the past twenty-four hours. I can't imagine how much worse it will get if the bombings continue for even one more day.*

School is supposed to be a place where children go to learn and play with their friends, not a shelter from violence and warfare. Mohamed and I conduct some interviews at the schools, and I play with the children. I speak to them, and take pictures and make videos with them. I try my best to make them smile, even just for a few minutes. In the midst of trauma, that's an accomplishment in and of itself.

It's only around noon, but I'm already tired from what I've seen, and I just want the day to be over. Mohamed decides to accompany me to Rasha's house, so I can briefly see my family – mama, teta and Judy. We only stay around ten minutes. We eat quickly, and I tell my mom that I signed a contract with an international news channel and that I've officially started working for them. I break the news that I'll be staying at Al-Quds indefinitely, because there's internet there, and cell service. Now that international news journalists aren't allowed into Gaza, reporting to these channels and getting the word out is crucial. She has no choice but to support me.

My teta has forgotten her medicine and her passport back

* Of course, a year later, they will still be ongoing.

at home, and mama asks me if it's possible for me to go grab them. It's a dangerous task, but I don't really think about that – I just go.

The streets are empty and quiet, with only the sound of bombings here and there in the distance. Everyone has evacuated the area. Mohamed and I go to my building as quickly as possible, covertly dash inside, grab the medicine and passport, and rush back to the car. The relief we feel while driving away is immense.

We need the internet. After delivering the medicine and passport, we make our way back to the office, and there's a connection – a weak one, but I can't complain. The video I filmed (the one where my jaw dropped as I heard the bombs in the background) is still going viral. Almost every news outlet in the world has posted it, and it's being translated into languages I haven't even heard of before. I'm astounded by the reaction; all I can do is hope that it's making a difference.

I'm just trying to check the news and upload a couple of videos. As I'm going through my messages, replying to what I can, I realize for the first time that the rest of the world is unaware that we don't have emergency shelters in Gaza. (Israel bans the entry of equipment that could be used to build them.) This blows my mind.

What did people think we were doing? How could they believe the odds were in any way fair?

It's going to get dark soon, and it's even more dangerous to move at night, so we have to leave the office. I call Ameer and tell him I'm on my way to Al-Quds. When I arrive, he gives me the keys to his office, because I have two live interviews to conduct and I can't find a single quiet corner at the hospital. It's full of displaced families and injured people, and has only gotten busier since my night staying there.

My phone is about to die and I can't find my charger. I think I left it in Mohamed's car, but I'm not sure. I start looking around the hospital for an iPhone cable, and I find myself back at the couch where I slept with my family. There's another family there now who let me borrow one; we become best friends as I wait for my battery to charge.

It turns out that they live in the same neighbourhood as me. We have a standing date to have lunch together after the Aggression. I hope I get to see them again. Their little girl's name is Dana. I haven't seen my Dana in weeks; I'm not used to being separated from her, especially when things are violent.

I ask the family if I can sleep in the same corner as them. The mom, Hana'a, tells her daughter to give me her pillow and to share her blanket.

I don't accept the pillow, but I gratefully share the blanket. The whole interaction means the world to me. A family I'd just met, who have lost everything themselves, want to share with me everything they had. It just sums up the Palestinian people in one gesture.

I sleep every night terrified of what tomorrow will bring. Today, Gazan hospital officials issue an international SOS, reporting that generator capacity is on course to run out.

It's only a matter of time before our health system collapses. Tick tock.

Day 6 | THURSDAY 12 OCTOBER

It's first thing in the morning, and Mohamed has come to pick me up from the hospital.

I run into Leen, the little girl I used to tutor, with her dad.

She insists that I come have breakfast with her family. Even though Mohamed is waiting for me, I run upstairs and greet her sister Lara, her brother Khalid and her mom Heba. Even in the middle of an Aggression, etiquette endures!

Her younger brother is injured, and my heart breaks a little bit. While the family were fleeing down the street, evacuating their grandparents' house, a missile struck his leg. They live a block away from Press House. I'm just grateful that they managed to secure a spot in the overcrowded hospital; it's a small relief amidst the chaos.

It is a good start to my day. It's always a pleasure to see people that I love dearly, no matter what the circumstances are. You take what you can get.

Mohamed and I start work. Our first mission is to interview a paramedic. This is my first time interviewing, or even speaking to, paramedics, and it's dawning on me how difficult their job truly is. They have to cope while Israel bombs the streets, blocking all their access routes and making it nearly impossible for them to reach anywhere. And their job is dangerous. Sometimes, Israel targets houses while people are still inside, injured, while the paramedics are trying to reach them through the bombing.

I keep getting flashbacks to 2021. I vividly remember when the IOF targeted a house in the Mushtaha complex, which is close to my home. From my mom's room, I could see how some apartments were catching fire after the bombing. When I asked mama why the firefighters hadn't arrived yet, she told me it was because they were still unsure if the target was just the burning apartments, or if Israel intended to bomb the whole complex. In Gaza, people's jobs are difficult in ways others can't imagine.

After the interviews, we decide to go back to Rasha's house. She has twins, Hoor and Osayd, who are both my sister's age and attend the same school as her. I feel like their older sibling. Just a couple of days before this, they were at our house, and I was forcing them to film TikToks with me. Judy and the twins sometimes study together, so I'm used to seeing them all the time; they're at our house almost daily, and we hang out with them at the weekends too. That's something about me – people don't need to be close to my age to be friends with me. I enjoy having relationships with people of wildly varying ages, because being friends with those older than me widens my horizon, and I get their wisdom and advice, while being friends with those younger than me basically means having teenagers fangirl over me.

Dana's the exception. She's only six months younger than me – not that I ever let her forget it. And now it's in a book, for ever.

We arrive at Rasha's house, which is basically a small villa. There's a garden at the entrance, and a small house, then another bigger house upstairs. Mohamed sits in the garden with Osama (Rasha's husband), and I go upstairs to where everyone else is. My timing is perfect – mama and Amal have just finished making pancakes – and I eat quickly. I try to appreciate them, because I'm not sure when I'll have pancakes again. Starvation is a common weapon of the Israeli forces.

I take a quick bath, and start on an expedition of borrowing clothes. I grab jeans and a white shirt from Hoor's closet, and a few black tees from Osayd's, because I want them oversized. I throw one on and give Mohamed another. I also grab some paracetamol, as the buzzing of the drones is giving me a headache, and then I say my goodbyes. It wasn't a long visit.

Mohamed and I continue working. We roam around Gaza, interviewing different people, asking them questions about the current situation. Most people are pessimistic, and afraid of what's yet to come. It makes sense. Al Jazeera is reporting that Israel has placed Gaza under a 'total siege', stopping food and fuel from reaching over two million people who are dependent on aid. We're only on day six.

Mohamed drops me off at Al-Quds before nightfall. I go to check on Leen, but I have to run because NBC wants to interview me. Leen and her sister Lara want to come, because they're bored, so I let them accompany me to the bombed-out house where I'm doing the interview, a five-minute walk from the hospital. The reporters end up interviewing Lara too, which I think is a good distraction for her. Because she's in middle school, they ask her about the future of education in Gaza, and she answers as we all would: how can I possibly know? The future is uncertain. We can't even envision what the next few days – or even hours – will be like.

After the interview, the girls keep me company while I roam around the hospital. I just keep staring at the eyes of those that we pass. It's becoming a melancholic habit.

Suddenly, the hospital is even more crowded than before. Doctors are in a state of panic and injured people start flooding in – lots of injured people, more than there are beds and far too many for the staff to deal with properly. Children are crying out in pain and adults are screaming in agony. I don't know what has happened, but the situation is dire. I try to help. I try to help identify unknown children, brought into the hospital by strangers who found them under rubble. I post about two of the kids on social media, and their relatives come to pick them up.

It turns out that a nearby building has been bombed. It's a surreal thing, being in a hospital during an emergency rush, especially one so graphic. Even though this isn't the first Aggression on Gaza, what's happening is like nothing I've experienced before. I don't know how I'll manage to stay sane.

Half an hour later, the vibe in the hospital starts to calm. But just when I think the day can't get any worse, I hear that Ameer has fainted. He isn't breathing and he's sweating heavily. My heart drops; for a minute, I think he's dying. He's not – it's just his body's reaction to grief. I learn that, today, Israel murdered Ameer's cousins.

I decide to go check on the family I met yesterday, then attempt to sleep before anything else bad happens. My brain thinks that if I close my eyes and sleep, so will the IOF. It's better to be killed in daylight anyway; it makes it easier for paramedics to identify you.

Going to see the family turns out to be a great decision. They're excited to see me, and they want to hear about my day. Then they start sharing stories of their lives in general. Hana'a coaches tennis, and she offers to teach me in exchange for Instagram advertising, after the Aggression. It's a great deal, and I'll hold her to it. We drink tea and follow the news, desperately hoping to hear something positive. We don't. Even so, I love the fact that we're making plans for after the Aggression. It gives me hope that it will end soon.

I want to end today on a positive note and say that I'm truly grateful for the people of Gaza. I believe the kindest people are the most powerful. I'm blessed that I know Leen and Lara, and that I got to spend some time with them today, and I'm blessed that I crossed paths with Hana'a and her family, and I'm blessed that they treat me like a family member they've known for years.

I end the day laughing hysterically. We are all trying to sleep but we can't. Then suddenly little Dana pipes up, saying that she can't get any rest because she is thinking about an injured donkey that she'd seen pictures of earlier in the day. I don't know why, but we all just burst out laughing. One voice tells her to try and sleep, while another sardonically mentions that she shouldn't feel bad for a donkey when she herself is displaced in a hospital – that one gets another roar out of everyone.

We all laugh for a good five minutes before we try to sleep once more, all of us with fear in our hearts over what is to come.

Day 7 | FRIDAY 13 OCTOBER

Sitting in a corner of a hospital,
Trying to write a poem.
But a child is crying.
A cat is wandering.
A young girl is screaming.
Doctors are panicking.
And the sound of bombs?
Only getting closer.

As the mother rocks her crying child,
Waiting for sleep to take his eyes,
He asks for time.
His mother, looking at the sky:
Two stars and a drone.
In the blink of an eye,
All that's left is
Darkness and drones.

I remain, sitting in the corner
Alone, with a spider
Trying to write a poem.

But it has already written itself.

I wake up to a notice from Israel, warning every Palestinian in North Gaza to flee to the south within twenty-four hours, which is nearly impossible. How are approximately 1.1 million people supposed to evacuate when there are barely any cars left working? We don't have any fuel. And where are we supposed to evacuate to? To a tent? Not everyone has family and friends in the south.

I leave the corner where I'm staying with Hana'a's family and go to wander around the hospital, trying to understand the situation and get a sense of what people are planning to do. Ironically, everyone starts asking *me* what they should do, and about my expectations as a journalist. I'm not wearing my gear, but I guess that's how people identify me now. They think I have some kind of secret access to information.

Little do they know that sometimes, they themselves are my secret access to information – the civilians. Yara called me the other day and asked me if a residential building had been bombed, and out of pure habit I told her to tell me more details, so I could post about it to inform people. She was fact-checking with me, not the other way around!

I flee my questioners by heading into Leen's family's room. They're confused and scared, especially given Khalid's injury. We then make a very Palestinian decision. We decide to take a break from panicking and have some breakfast together, given that it could be our last breakfast in North Gaza. Not for the first time, I'm grateful that the little falafel restaurant in front of the hospital has stayed open.

I don't know the falafel man, but he deserves respect. Chaos births unlikely heroes.

After a long discussion with Heba, I decide that I should go be with my family at Rasha's house. If we are to die, it's better for us all to die together, I think. And Heba decides that she's either going to stay at the hospital with her family and hope for the best, or go to her parents, who are refusing to leave their house, also in the north, if she can.

We sit together quietly, until Leen's dad breaks the silence: 'If we die,' he says, 'this is an honourable death.'

This sentence is the final straw. I break down. I have been trying to hold back my tears ever since the evacuation order – I'm a journalist; if I start crying, people panic even more, so I need to keep it together – but after Leen's dad said that, the floodgates opened. It was all too real and everything started to hit me.

I leave their room after a time, and I go downstairs to check for cell service. I've been trying to call my mom and Mohamed, but my calls aren't going through.

More people are coming into the hospital than are leaving – they don't know where to go or what to do. I see Ameer and he tells me that, as long as there are patients and people inside, the Palestine Red Crescent will be staying where they are – and that if there's an evacuation, they'll be the last ones to leave.

One thing about me is that I rarely cry, but if I start crying, I can't stop. I kept seeing displaced people arriving at the hospital, and everyone is asking me endless questions that I can't answer. I still can't reach my mom or Mohamed or Hatem, but I have the internet so my phone is blowing up with interview requests and messages. I feel so overwhelmed and I cry for more than thirty minutes. I am stuck in a hospital, waiting for a collective death. And, honestly, I never wanted to die displaced in a hospital.

Motaz Azaiza, a fellow journalist I met on Instagram before all this started, shows up from somewhere, and we film a video together, just talking about how bad the situation is getting, and how clueless we are about what the million-plus people in North Gaza are supposed to do right now. We initially connected with plans for a photoshoot by the sea, but instead now we're filming videos together about displacement. At least it's a distraction.

I keep trying to reach Mohamed with no luck. I try professional drivers that I know, but I either can't get through to them or they're already with their families, trying to evacuate themselves. Eventually, I get through to mama; I tell her that I'm looking for a taxi, and that I'm coming to her as soon as I can.

The situation in the hospital just keeps getting worse. I don't feel like working or vlogging or doing interviews. I'm so fed up with journalism; I'm questioning all my life decisions as I wait for death. The only thing running through my mind is that it's only a matter of time before Israel bombs North Gaza, and we all die.

Then I ask myself if this is how I want to spend what could be the last few hours of my life. And I take up my phone and I just start texting my friends. I take off my press vest and helmet, and I post a picture on Instagram, using my thoughts as a caption:

> I've always loved journalism, and Palestine, and I'm glad I was able to share part of the truth, or part of what's happening, with the world . . .
>
> I am still in the hospital. I tried to evacuate and go to where my parents are, but I can't find a car or a taxi and I need to like walk for an hour or more and I don't have energy and my back hurts a lot from wearing the press vest which I'm sure doesn't protect me from anything, but at least it makes me feel that I've done what I'm supposed to do to protect myself. Oh to add, I lost cellular connection, I can't call or send anyone a message, but there is still internet at the hospital so l can post this.
>
> There is still time before the night comes, I'll see if I'll have any options and I'll keep you updated if I can.
>
> *My DMs and WhatsApp will explode with messages for interviews, but obviously now is not a good time and it all feels pointless tbh, everything you need to know is already on my Instagram.

Shortly after I post, my mom's cousin calls me and tells me that there's a white taxi waiting for me outside, and that I'd better hurry or he'll leave. I grab my stuff, say goodbye to everyone as quickly as I can, and go. I don't have the chance to update my social media, and I'm grateful to the cousin because he says he'll update mama.

I am shocked by what I see in the streets on the way to Rasha's house. People are just walking, walking, walking, carrying their lives in their bags with them. I see the 1948 Nakba in front of my eyes, just as my grandfather once described it to me. I remember him telling me how he was forcibly displaced from his home, and how Israel's goal was to ethnically cleanse Palestine of Palestinians. And here I was, seeing it for myself. Where are all these people supposed to go?

I arrive at Rasha's, and I pay the taxi driver a triple fare. It's basic economics: when demand is high and supply is low, prices increase. Even during an Aggression. But I don't complain about it; I'm beyond lucky to be able to find a car.

I finally reunite with my family, and I spend the rest of the day flitting between a restless sleep and spending time with them. I'm tired, and I feel sick with unease. There's no internet and barely any service. I'm done.

Day 8 | SATURDAY 14 OCTOBER

I wake up feeling famous today. Khalo calls and says that he's seen my Instagram.

You know how, in every family, there's that one cool member who lives abroad and always goes on vacations? The one that all the younger members look up to? In my family, that's Khalo Khaled, my mom's youngest brother ('khalo' means 'maternal uncle'). While mama was already married and having kids, khalo was studying for a master's degree in Egypt, and he'd always come back to Gaza bringing us gifts. The day after his visits, I'd go to school and feel like I was in a fashion show, modelling all the stuff he'd bought me.

Then he graduated, started working and basically grew up. He married a woman named Reeman in Jordan in 2014. We didn't get to attend the wedding – we were planning to, but an Aggression started and the borders closed. At this point, the last time I had seen him was in 2021, when I visited him in Dubai. I was eighteen years old, and still a university student. He was still the cool uncle. Nothing had changed. Until . . .

He tells us that my social media is blowing up with followers, and that everyone in the comments is asking whether I'm dead or alive. He urges me to try to connect to the internet, to update my feed. I explain to him that I can't get any connection, and that I'm still not able to reach any of my colleagues to understand the situation more clearly. I don't even know if they're still working or not.

Stepping back from the horrible reality for a second, I realize I've kind of become the cool one in the family. Sorry, khalo, your days are numbered. Now my cousins can say their cousin reports live from an Aggression. I'm kidding, obviously, but you can't deny that being a journalist in Gaza is objectively more interesting than being an orthodontist in Dubai.

I'm happy about my fame for approximately seven seconds. Then reality starts hitting me. Is this my life now? Being displaced in a friend's house with a sore back? Will I ever be able to reach any of my colleagues and report again, or will I just be trapped in this place that isn't even mine? Honestly, I thought that I'd be killed by now; a part of me can't believe I'm still alive.

At least there's food to eat. And I eventually reach Mohamed. He's busy evacuating his family, but he's been trying to reach me as well. I give him my location and tell him to come by tomorrow if he can. We can plan how we might work then.

Day 9 | SUNDAY 15 OCTOBER

In the Gaza Strip, we don't have the luxury of planning our days. You can try to plan if you want to, but Israel will have its own agenda. On day nine, my plan for the day is to get back to work with Mohamed. It is pretty simple. Wake up, have Mohamed pick me up, work, then have Mohamed drop me back at Rasha's. What could go wrong?

I can't get a hold of Mohamed. It has been hours and I don't know if he's okay.

He eventually shows up when it's close to nightfall. He wasn't able to work all morning. There was a problem with the car wheels because the streets are full of rubble and rocks. So he spent half of his day searching for a place to fix the car, and the second half searching for gas for it. We agree that we'll try again the next day, except he'll bring Hatem with him. And the three of us will work together from now on.

I spend that evening explaining to mama that once I leave for work, I won't be coming back to Rasha's. Mohamed and

I have decided that I will base myself out of the house of one of my extended family members in Khan Younis.

In Palestine, most families have incredibly close relationships with one another. Usually, parents build their sons' houses above their own, and each son moves in once he gets married, and so it is with my grandparents' house in Khan Younis. My grandparents live on the ground floor, and there are three extensions above them for my uncles and my dad. There's no furniture in dad's section, because mama works in Gaza City, and teta lives there too. With baba working abroad and my brother Ahmed studying in Canada, it made sense to stay there.

My brother is a year older than me, but I graduated before him because I'm smarter. Ahmed is chill to the point that it annoys me. I live life as if I'm in a race with time, whereas he's off living life as if he's a ballerina, spinning through the world without a care. He doesn't care when he graduates. It could take four or five years, and it's all fine by him. All that matters to him is that eventually he will graduate, and work, and go through the same life cycle as everyone else, so why the rush?

He's even like that when he's going out. If we're running out of time, you'll find me running around the house looking for this and that, while Ahmed strolls around like a TORTOISE because – here's that phrase again – why the rush? It's not the end of the world if we're late! His words, not mine. Now, enough talking about Ahmed. He's chill but he hates when people talk about him. He prefers something called 'privacy', a concept I have yet to relate to or understand. Oops.

My mother is scared for me to leave her. I tell her that people in Gaza are afraid of the IOF specifically targeting journalists, and that I don't want anyone to feel as though they have to put their own lives in danger in order to host me – and that includes Rasha, even if she's a dear friend. I can trust my uncles in Khan Younis when they tell me that they understand, and are proud of my career and my bravery (their words, not mine). They're not just displaying etiquette. Plus, Khan Younis is supposed to be safer than here in the north, at least according to the IOF.

My sister helps me convince my mom that I should go, saying that it's essential for my work. Judy's a seventeen-year-old who just wants to flex to her friends that her sister is a famous journalist working on the ground – she's completely delusional – but I don't care. She's supporting the cause.

In the end, my mom doesn't have any option but to agree to my plan. What else is she supposed to do? If I stay here, I'll only nag her about not working, possibly making her life more miserable than Israel ever could.

My mom's a smart woman. She makes the right decision.

Day 10 | MONDAY 16 OCTOBER

I wake up to the sound of a car horn beeping. It's Mohamed and Hatem. I dress quickly, grabbing my press vest and helmet. I say goodbye to anyone who's awake, and I leave. I know an unpredictable day is waiting for me.

Priority number one, aside from not getting killed, is connecting to the internet so I can update my Instagram. We go to Shuhada Al-Aqsa Hospital in Deir Al-Balah, where there's a 'Journalist Zone' out front. Journalists can work, charge their phones and get limited internet access. It's nothing fancy – it's just the corner of a street with a few chairs set up, and lots of cameras and journalists – but I'm grateful for it.

I quickly film an update for my followers. I tell them I'm alive and that I haven't had internet access for two days. I post it without checking my messages (I don't have time), then immediately join Mohamed inside the hospital. We have to work when we can. He starts filming, and it's my job to conduct interviews. It's usually a special skill of mine, but sometimes I'm too stunned to ask the right questions. There's barely enough space for me to walk through the hospital. It's overcrowded, with displaced and injured people lining the corridors; there aren't enough beds for everyone. I think I should start getting used to seeing this in hospitals.

Later, my friend's mother calls me and, in a devastated voice, tells me to check social media – specifically X. The Israeli propaganda machine has turned against me, and is scrutinizing my necklace. It has been passed down through my family. My teta gave it to my mom, and mama gave it to me a couple of years before this Aggression started. I'm always wearing it. It's in the shape of Palestine, and inside there's an engraving of the Palestinian flag and the word 'Palestine' written in Arabic. It's beautiful, and special to me.

They're claiming that I'm not a journalist, and that I'm actually a member of Hamas. Zionists and Israelis are posting about my necklace, characterizing it as the 'annihilate Israel' necklace. I don't even know what they mean.

What on earth does 'annihilate Israel' mean in the context I am in?! In Gaza, the healthcare system is on the verge of completely breaking down. Health officials are using ice-cream freezer trucks to store the bodies of Palestinians killed in air strikes. It is too dangerous to transport them back to hospitals and there is no space left in the cemeteries and morgues. UN-OCHA has reported that fuel reserves at all hospitals across Gaza are projected to last only twenty-four hours before depletion.

I keep writing that the situation is getting worse but it is. I just don't understand how Israelis have the ability to twist the truth of what is happening, nor why the rest of the world seemingly believes them. Israel gaslights – it acts like you're a hysterical woman, when, really, it's just a toxic man, flipping the table on you and telling you you're wrong to ever question it.

I try to distract myself from the horrors around me, like the fact that there are still Palestinians missing under the rubble, or that there's a huge shortage of medical supplies. I focus on my face. It's red, and parts of my body are too. I think it's some kind of rash. And it's really itchy! I can feel myself wanting to scratch myself while I'm talking to people, but I don't want them to think I'm mangy. And I can't talk to a doctor about it – they're all off dealing with amputations and burns and other severe injuries. I would feel so ridiculous taking a doctor's time to talk about a rash.

I guess I'll just live with it.

I go back to my grandparents' house in Khan Younis, and I spend the evening chatting with my cousins until we sleep.

Plestia Alaqad

Day 11 | TUESDAY 17 OCTOBER

I wake up every day, if I was able to sleep, not knowing what to expect.

I've developed a kind of routine. Mohamed and Hatem pick me up, and we start our uncertain day in Gaza together. We spend half the day reporting, and the other half searching for things that should always be available.

Food. Water. Shelter.

Life's basic necessities. What every human and animal needs to survive. Today, in Gaza, having any of the three is a luxury and a privilege. To drink water, you have to stand for hours in a line. To find food, you have to search through depleted markets and hope you find something affordable. And shelter? You're either lucky enough to know someone who's still living in a house, or you're fortunate and you find a tent somewhere. If you don't, you sleep in your car. Or your friend's car. And you try not to move around, because gas is difficult to find and more expensive than usual. So displacement zones end up forming – for example, the backyard of Al-Shifa Hospital is full of tents and cars being used as shelter right now. I don't want this to become a normal scene. I refuse to accept that this is my life now.

The Strip has always been overpopulated, but people are usually spread out across different areas. Now, with the IOF continually asking Palestinians to evacuate their homes, certain areas are getting dangerously overcrowded. Israel bombed Al-Maamdani Baptist Hospital today. It's the first time they've directly targeted a hospital. I hope that Dr Ghassan – a plastic and reconstructive surgeon there – is physically okay. If doctors start getting hurt, then who will take care of the injured people? I met Dr Ghassan on the fourth or fifth day of the Aggression at Al-Shifa. I instantly noticed his courage and the care he took for his patients. He impressed me. I've already made it a habit to go check on him whenever we are near a hospital he is at. If I am exhausted from reporting and in a crap mood, Dr Ghassan will instantly cheer me up. Suddenly I won't be tired any more. He's that kind of guy. And now he might be dead.

The trauma in Gaza is multilayered. I no longer know what to shed light on, what to write about or what to feel, whether as a Palestinian journalist or as a human. The IOF killed hundreds of people at Al-Maamdani, mostly women and children; Dr Ghassan told me he saw legs and hands alone, bodiless, in the backyard of the hospital. I cannot understand why they would target a hospital full of the injured and the displaced. It seems there are no red lines.

I'm embarrassed to say it out loud, but a part of me is happy that Al-Maamdani got bombed, because that might mean the end of the Aggression. After you strike a hospital, where do you go from there? What else is left for you to destroy? Which lives are left for you to target?

I hope I wake up tomorrow and it's all over.

Day 12 | WEDNESDAY 18 OCTOBER

I wake up and it isn't all over.

Today, the 'war' ended. This isn't an Aggression any more; it's a Genocide. There isn't another word that can describe the scale of violence I see in front of me.

Plestia Alaqad

I start the day at Al-Maamdani, which was bombed yesterday. Yet another healthcare facility, yet another critical service for human survival, destroyed by the IOF. I can see where the missile landed. It's obvious. I can see all the damage, the broken glass of the windows strewn across the courtyard, the cars that are burned out and abandoned. I see other journalists holding back tears and taking deep breaths, trying to compose themselves before gathering up the power to film their reports. I see people who were witness to the massacre yesterday; I wish I could say that they're empty shells, that they've been afforded even the luxury of being in a state of shock, but they're not. They're practical, and broken, and they're here to look for their stuff.

There's a church here. People's belongings are still where they left them. I see a sandwich on the floor, with just one bite taken out of it, and my thoughts fly to the person who was eating it. They were a displaced civilian, camping out in the church of a hospital, hungry and trying to survive. And at best, they had to flee when the bombing started, forced to respond to their fear before their starvation. Maybe they later died, hungry and left for dust by the rest of the world – a world that still stands by, complacent, allowing the Israelis to get away with Genocide.

Because that's what it is now. The world can't pretend that there are two sides here any more. There is no humanity, no equity, no semblance of justice. It's a calculated, deliberate and ruthless ethnic cleansing, and nobody seems to care enough.

Why do we live in a world where Genocide has been normalized? I spot a baby bottle in the church, under the rubble, full of milk. What happened to that baby? And its parents, what did they tell her? That this is what a thunderstorm sounds like?

Yesterday, there were hundreds of displaced people taking shelter in this courtyard. They had nowhere else to go, and they thought that a hospital would be the safest place. Imagine yourself in their shoes. You're displaced, living in a tent in a yard, and, with no notice, Israel fires a missile directly at you. Most of the time, they strike you with a drone, a machine from afar, branded with a US arms dealer's logo. And then you either die, or live to see others murdered and mutilated, with amputated limbs. And that's your life.

I go to Al-Shifa next; it's overcrowded too, with the displaced and injured strewn around like wreckage from a ship, floating wherever they can find any kind of buoyancy. I enter the hospital searching for Dr Ghassan. To my relief, I've found out that he is unharmed, and I'm here to interview him as an eyewitness to yesterday's massacre.

Everything is starting to trigger a cascade of emotions in me. There are items of clothing hanging on bannisters around the hospital, and I begin to imagine the story behind each one. I see a little purple dress and I think of how at one time it was probably a little girl's Eid outfit, to be worn on happy days, and how it's now her displacement uniform. I see a man's formal shirt – maybe that was her dad's work outfit, and maybe he's dead now.

Mohamed's voice interrupts my imagination. 'We've arrived. Dr Ghassan is inside this room.' I'm nervous – what am I supposed to ask a doctor who's been eyewitness to a massacre *inside* a hospital? – but he immediately puts me at ease. Despite the layers of trauma visible through his eyes, he has the ability to make a person feel comfortable without saying a word. The interview proceeds; it's sad, but it comes off without a hitch.

After the interview wraps up, I decide that I can't live with the itchiness of my rash for ever, so I ask him for his advice. He tells me that it is just my anxiety showing on my face, and he gives me a cream. I feel a bit bad asking Dr Ghassan – a man who is dealing with amputee and wounded children on a daily basis at the time – about a minor skin condition. But he doesn't seem to mind. I guess we both need a distraction after a conversation about how to go about finding kids' amputated limbs in a bombed-out courtyard.

Afterwards, Mohamed, Hatem and I go searching for some food and an internet connection, to upload our work. Outside isn't much better than inside. People are trying to go about their daily lives. In a Genocide, that means just trying to survive and salvage whatever you can. There's a long queue of people lined up behind a well, trying to fill their water canisters. There's a man in his forties standing in the street with some clothes to sell – I assume he had a store, it got bombed and he saved what he could to try to make some money.

I manage to find some popcorn in the market, and I take it 'home' to my family. We usually eat popcorn on movie nights. That's another thing that has been stolen from me – will I ever sit with my family and eat popcorn while watching a movie again? The whole evening, I'm zoned out. It's like my life has become the movie, but it's a movie that should never have been made, a movie that I'd never watch but somehow find myself a leading character in. The innocent bystander. Is what's happening even real? Is this my reality now?

One thing I like about myself is my ability to un-sync my head and my heart. Every day, my heart aches for the trauma and pain I see around me, and I want to cry, but my brain tells me that I don't have time for that. I have to report on what's happening; it's the only way I can possibly help. So I tell my heart to pause, and I just listen to what my brain tells me to do.

And that's what I do. Day after day after day. Autopilot. I continue to eat popcorn, sharing stories with my family about what I saw earlier today.

Day 13 | THURSDAY 19 OCTOBER

I asked my friend
Can't you postpone your crying?

He answered, with tear-filled eyes:
No, I don't have time to cry tomorrow.

Life is a race,
And I am tired
Of chasing time
That kills everything left in me.

Time is chasing me, and I am chasing it.
I can't stop to catch my breath,
Because it never stops.

I told time: I am tired too,
Of waiting for things that never comes to pass,
For mail that doesn't arrive,
And phones that don't ring.

Time is killing every hope within me.

I now pause a lot and stare at everything and wonder if it will be the last time I see it. I drink water, and I stop before my thirst is sated, because I don't know when I'll be able to find water easily again. I take a picture of the water bottle, thinking it might be a memory soon. I don't leave the house without taking the time to look at each member of my family, trying to absorb as much as I can about them, in case I never can again.

We start the day looking for gas. By the time we find a station that's still stocked, the line of people outside it is down the street. But when we tell them we're journalists, people let us cut the queue. Then we go looking for bread. Another line, in fact, two: one for men and one for women. Both are endless. People actually spend hours buying bread nowadays; that's part of their day. Sometimes it runs out just when it's your turn.

It's a nightmare. I think the time it takes to get basic necessities in a Genocide is overlooked, but it's absolutely the daily experience of living through one. The queues are long, people are hungry and tired, and the feeling of frustration around not being able to buy something as simple as bread is a whole trauma of its own. I spent half of the day – half of my actual day – looking for gas and carbs. No human will accept that as a normal situation, no matter what's going on around them.

Eventually, we go to an UNRWA school near the Rafah border crossing. It's mostly full of those lucky enough to have dual nationalities; they're waiting for their governments to put their name on a list that will mean they can immediately leave Gaza once the Rafah borders are open again. We spend our time chatting with them, sharing our fears of uncertainty and further trauma with one another.

The school is full of stories of people who came to visit Gaza after years of exile – those who were forced to flee in 1967 or during an Aggression – and who got stuck after the Genocide started. I meet an elderly couple (I say elderly; they are like fifty, but they have grandchildren, so that makes them elderly in my mind) who are in Palestine for the first time in decades, having been driven out by the very Israelis who are now keeping them constrained and locked in. They are worried about their children, because they don't have any service or internet connection to tell them that they are safe. They tell me that they think their kids probably believe they're dead. That is a whole new layer of trauma I've never considered before.

I understand that documentation is important, and I'll never discount the value of sharing with the world what's happening here, but today I mostly just sit and listen to people without recording or filming. They're terrified. Terrified of everything. And they don't always need a journalist shoving a camera in their face. I respect their fear. What has the international press ever done for them? So I sit, and I listen, and I try to give them some kind of outlet through which they can be heard.

As usual, people we meet think that we know everything, because we're journalists and we're kept up to date. But we don't even have internet access. Nevertheless, people keep asking us about the borders, about whether they're open or if there's any humanitarian aid coming through. We go to check, but the crossing is closed.

We do find something positive, however. There's a cafeteria that's still somehow open, and we manage to get our hands on some cookies. COOKIES! I never thought I'd be this happy over cookies but here I am. There are as many firsts as there are lasts. We put some of them away in our car, in case of emergency, and we each bring back a portion for our families too.

After a long day, I have a blessed moment of peace at my uncle's house with my family – today, mama, teta and Judy left Al-Zahra and came to join me in Khan Younis. We brew some tea, and we dip the cookies in it, and they try to give me space before they start asking me for updates. But they have to ask. Gaza is small, but anybody who doesn't leave their house (or tent) can quickly start to feel isolated, because there isn't any internet or cell service available, and the collective feeling of fear is like a plague hanging around the streets.

So, I take a deep breath, set aside my tea and the crumbs of joy that I've managed to cling to today, and I start my report in earnest.

Day 14 | FRIDAY 20 OCTOBER

I think I have a new superpower – I can function without sleep.

With everything that's been happening, I've barely gotten any rest. Most nights, when I close my eyes, I can't help but relive the stories of all the people I've spoken to. The sound of crying babies haunts me. The images of injured and amputee kids live rent free in my head. Nowadays, I often wonder which is better, consciousness or sleep. Both are a nightmare, and I don't know which one is real.

Every day, I try to rest, and every day I open my eyes to even more devastating news. Israel is only outdoing itself with its crimes, as if it's taking part in some sick, twisted *Hunger Games*-type scenario where the more brutality it can show, the higher its viewer ratings will be. And, in a way, Netanyahu is playing that game. What seems to be constantly overlooked by sections of the Western media is the political power that he stands to gain from the Genocide. We're so often told that his country has the 'right to defend itself', but it's not protection that's giving him power with the ministers he has surrounded himself with in his government, it's aggression. Aggressions always lead to better politics for the Israelis behind them – they're the motor behind their political progress.

Yesterday night, Israeli warplanes targeted the Church of St Porphyrius. According to eyewitnesses, seventeen people were killed and there are more victims buried under the rubble, not yet identified. That's our first stop of the day.

It's still early in the morning when Mohamed, Hatem and I arrive. The trauma and devastation are clear on everyone's faces. Men are desperately trying to search for survivors under the rubble, but they're only finding more victims – I see them extract the body of a baby, his life cut short at mere months. There are Christmas decorations buried underneath the carnage too, and I get a stabbing reminder of just how much Israel is ruining our lives. This church has stood for almost 900 years.*

There's a dad here who's the only survivor from his family. His two children and his wife were killed in the bombing. There aren't any words for what I see in his eyes. They're broken, and full of conflicting emotions. He's never going to be the same person again. Is it normal that a part of me wishes he got killed too? I don't want him to have to live, and to have to experience this sort of death for the sake of life.

My friend Yara's family have been staying in this church. I run into Bader, her brother, who's assisting with the recovery effort. By sheer luck, their dad had thought to evacuate them

* They will attack it again in July 2024, as people camp in the wreckage.

to another church a couple of days before St Porphyrius was attacked. Nobody in Gaza is alive through anything other than sheer luck. But I experience a heartening moment, because Bader is here and he's helping people; in Gaza, we're just one big family, bonded by trauma. That's all there is.

We're still reporting on the attack when we hear bombing coming from outside. The Israelis have targeted a small building nearby with a warning missile – not enough to destroy the structure, but enough to cause panic and alert people to the likelihood of another, bigger bomb incoming shortly afterwards. How humane.

I hate the warning missiles. They're scarier than the actual bombing, because they create more chaos. When the missile hits the building, people start to scramble, terrified, through the streets, unsure of where to go or whether to walk or run. We see a mom struggling to deal with two young girls who are crying, both because they are afraid but also because they've forgotten their slippers in their home and it isn't safe for them to go back and grab them. The mom is also petrified, desperately trying to keep her daughters calm as they all wait for her husband and son, who are still scavenging through their house for valuables and important documents, to join them.

We watch them for maybe a minute. One minute. And, in that minute, we witness a lifetime of emotions pass over the mom's face. I see her worrying that her husband and son won't make it back alive, questioning whether a piece of paper is worth their lives, convincing herself that they will be bombed and murdered while trying to salvage the remnants of their lives.

We go to stand with them. We shouldn't. We should run away and leave the area, because the IOF are going to bomb exactly where we are standing at any minute. But we stay. We can't leave them alone. We make sure that the dad and son make it out alive, and then we all run away together. Mohamed takes the mom's contact details, and we promise them that we'll come back to them with slippers for the girls.

As we are driving away in the car, we can hear the sound of bombing behind us, and we feel safe once again. As long as you can hear the sound of bombs, you're safe.

Because you'll never hear the rocket that kills you.

We move on towards Al-Shifa Hospital, to gather some more footage for our report on the bombing there. On our way, we stop at an UNRWA camp in Khan Younis and I consider for a moment how the Genocide has twisted things in my mind. I always thought of camping as something fun and exciting. Tents meant friends, bonfires, marshmallows and sing-songs. But nobody's singing now. Camping is our reality, but tents are sad, and cold, and empty.

It's a different type of pain, to see your homeland, once covered with olive and lemon trees, lush, fruitful pastures and the remnants of ancient, beautiful humanity, reduced to rubble, populated by camps and tents. I can't always gather the strength to film what I see, because my eyes don't want to believe that what they see is true. So instead, I just walk through the camp, between the tents, watching people's eyes and trying to memorize their faces, so that somebody will have known them before the end.

The Palestinian flag hoisted outside Al-Shifa is dripping with blood, but it continues to blow in the wind, refusing to allow itself to be weighed down. This is what Palestinians are like; this is what the people of Gaza are going through. We're tired. Our features have changed. We have all lost loved ones.

But we wake up, every day, and we try to survive.

Day 15 | SATURDAY 21 OCTOBER

It's day fifteen, if I'm not mistaken. Time is not passing.

Humanitarian aid trucks enter Gaza for the first time today. But what relief are twenty trucks when you have an entire city that's starving? And what point had we reached that I was expected to feel grateful for them? What did I ever do wrong to be put in such a position?

I've always loved writing and journaling, but I like documenting happy moments. And yet here I am living through a Genocide. I feel I have to show the world the truth, but that's difficult to do while I'm also trying to stay alive.

It's insane to me how people across the globe are experiencing second-hand trauma from coverage of the Genocide online. I receive their messages, I see their posts and I want to feel buoyed. I want to feel lifted up, and believe that the world is finally waking up to the plight of the Palestinians but I can't. What's being covered by media outlets, and being posted on social media platforms, makes up about 10 per cent of the actual situation on the ground in Gaza.

The most harrowing stories are left unreported. People in Palestine have lost faith in the media, and how can I blame them? Two stories with exactly the same factual details, one from Kyiv and one from Gaza, are treated entirely differently by the news. It's difficult to believe in impartial journalism when facts and narratives have been weaponized and distorted, and lies and propaganda have found stable ground. There's a practical reason too – people in Gaza are actively dealing with sketchy internet and power cuts, as well as shortages of fuel, medicine and food. Would you bother trying to tell the truth to an audience that doesn't listen, or would you just try to survive?

I see more and more bombed-out houses and buildings every day, which means that there are more displaced people than ever. People are evacuating to schools, universities and hospitals, which are not places suitable for humans to live in. The IOF has targeted our homes, our mosques, even our ambulances. What else will they destroy?

The saddest thing is that I'm losing my ability to react, out of tiredness. I am so drained, just like everybody else. I want this nightmare to end, but I'm also afraid of what life will look like once it does. Will there even be a Gaza still? I'm terrified of the aftermath. And there's nobody to question, nobody to reassure me that there's a plan. Israel has deliberately destroyed every pillar that we have.

Even writing, my therapy, isn't working. Nothing makes me feel better.

Day 16 | SUNDAY 22 OCTOBER

We saw a jujube tree today while we were out reporting, and Hatem grabbed some of its fruit. We ate them without washing them, because we didn't want to waste our water.

During week one, when I thought it was a 'normal'

Aggression, I would wash everything before eating it – and lowkey judge the others for not doing the same. But it has become a Genocide, and the opposite has started happening. I wash nothing, and judge anyone who doesn't think the same.

Unless they experience it first-hand, nobody can understand what it's like to live in the midst of an active Genocide. Humans aren't supposed to naturally understand, let alone cope with, the mindset that they might be alive one minute and burned, injured or killed the next. You don't get used to that.

I've been thinking about it, and I don't think surviving is everything. For example, I think I'd rather die than live with a severely burned face. That's not what the Hollywood hero should say, but I've personally seen the trauma and the emotional scarring that can happen to someone after their face is taken away from them. It's something core to our identities and how we see ourselves, compose ourselves, live with ourselves. I like my face and how I look and, more importantly, I'm used to it.

There isn't a lot of solid ground around you when it's all being bombed. So yes, please, at least I'd like to keep my face. (If it was severely injured, though, I'd want Dr Ghassan to fix it.)

Day 17 | MONDAY 23 OCTOBER

Mohamed and I are in the car, roving the streets of Gaza, when we see a house get bombed. We stop to report on the story and interview the residents, but we end up helping them instead. We search with the family who have lost their home, digging under the rubble, trying to salvage anything. Literally anything. A picture. A document. An outfit. A doll. Anything to give them their identities back.

On a daily basis, I'm torn between my role as a journalist – reporting on the Genocide, spreading the message of my people to the world – and existing as a Palestinian. How can I not help them search the rubble, how can I not extend that kindness, when I know that they wouldn't hesitate to do the same for me?

Amidst all of the chaos, we have an important mission for the day. Today, we have to help Hatem. His house was partially demolished in an airstrike overnight. His son Hani (nickname: Aloos) is distressed, and crying out for a small plant which was in their home. He had been working on it for a school project, and he really wants to see it grow.

So we all go to what's left of Hatem's house, to try to save the plant.

It's this kind of stuff, isn't it? Little, everyday impulses that shatter my heart into a million pieces. This kid is just a little boy, only seven or eight years old. Imagine his mindset. Bombs are flying, people are dying and his whole world is coming down around him, and he doesn't want to leave his plant, something he helped grow and keep alive, behind.

Children will be children, no matter the circumstances. Hatem's son isn't able to comprehend the scale of the violence and destruction around him, and it is entirely natural for him to focus only on what he feels he can control. The plant is still important to him, because it is a part of the world that someone has given to him and told him he could care for. It is the sweetest, most bitter feeling when he insists, with all the might of a hero from folklore, that we try to save it.

Who knows? Maybe the real truth is that eight-year-old children shouldn't have to think like he has to; maybe they should be left with their innocence for a little bit longer. But it makes me think: if this little boy won't leave a school project behind, how could we ever expect him to leave his land? How could we justify it to him?

I'm glad we go back for the plant.

I don't really want to write about anything other than saving Aloos's plant, because for me that is all that matters today – but there is one other highlight. We find ice cream! How did we manage that in a city without any electricity or basic necessities? Well, we find a small market and there is a kid coming out eating a red ice lolly, so we immediately go inside. Turns out, the shopkeeper still has a few ice creams left, and electricity from a solar generator. He is selling them before they inevitably get ruined. It is amazing.

I take so many pictures of that ice cream. I don't know – it felt like an event, eating ice cream in the middle of a Genocide.

Day 18 | TUESDAY 24 OCTOBER

I'm back. I know that I said that writing doesn't make me feel better any more, but what else should I do? Who else can I talk to?

Today is a heavy day. Every day feels like the worst day of my life, then Israel outdoes itself and the next day is worse. My existence is an increasingly suffocating nightmare.

Gaza is no longer recognizable. I walk the streets and all I can see is destruction. The health system is collapsing; today, the Indonesian Hospital lost all power, and its vital facilities were disrupted when it ran out of fuel. People were on life support. And that's not even the worst news of the day – I mean, how can a person decide what the worst news of the day is any more? I learn that over the past twenty-four hours, Israel has killed over 700 Palestinians, bringing the total to 5,791 people murdered since 7 October.

More than half of them are children.

More than half of them are children.

MORE THAN HALF OF THEM ARE CHILDREN!

If I scream it loud enough, will the world hear me?

Today I interview Dr Ghassan. He's an inspiration, even though he only has bad news for me – he tells me that Al-Shifa has admitted over 400 people in the last twenty-four hours, because Israel is bombing areas close to the hospital, and that those 400 people have completely overwhelmed an already drowning healthcare system. It's not a good picture. Still, just seeing him gives me hope. He is always willing to speak to journalists like me. I still don't understand how he has the time to give to both his patients and the media. His relationship with those in his care is unlike any other doctor–patient relationship I've ever seen. He knows all their names. He remembers every child he has ever treated.

I know personally how overwhelming media work can be, especially when you've been repeating yourself for weeks and you feel that nobody is listening, and no change is happening. Yet, somehow, Dr Ghassan is resilient. He keeps sharing the truth with the world, trying his best regardless of how muted the response is.

I'm tired, and all I wish is for life to go back to normal, even though I don't know what that means to a Palestinian in Gaza any more.

While I was living it, I never thought a day would come where I'd wish for my previous life back, exactly as it was – and yet here I am. With a Genocide unfolding right in front of me, I'd give anything to be triggered by teta's radio.

Day 19 | WEDNESDAY 25 OCTOBER

It is 10 a.m., and my mom, Judy, teta and my other family members are still sleeping. Mohamed and Hatem will be here to pick me up any minute. We will try our best to keep going, to continue reporting on what's happening, and we will hope not to die.

I keep having discussions with myself about my death. It's weird, because they're getting more pragmatic. There's less wondering about an afterlife and more considering the practicalities that would follow it. I hope that I come back to my family in one piece, even if I'm dead. I don't want to be cut up, or blasted into a million pieces. But regardless, I would want them to be proud. At least, if I die, I want to be satisfied that I was doing what I truly believe in right up until the very last minute.

I find it hard to sleep at night. I wake up from terrible nightmares to an even scarier reality. I'm terrified that anything might happen to me at any minute. Growing up in Gaza, it was natural to imagine what living through a Genocide might be like, but what's happening has exceeded even my most despairing expectations. And I have a particularly wild imagination!

But fear doesn't paralyse me. It pushes me forward, not backwards. Fear is the motivation.

I make it back home alive. Yay to physically surviving another day.

Day 20 | THURSDAY 26 OCTOBER

It's day twenty, and I am not used to this. I don't think anyone is. I don't think anyone could be. I wake up every day and wonder if it will be my last.

I feel selfish that I'm able to drink water or eat, when I know that others – my people – cannot. I'm scared of what life will be like when all this ends. I keep thinking about wounded men, and widowed women, and orphaned children. I keep thinking about the little boy who keeps waiting, desperately, for his mama to come back to life, or the man who has been searching for days under the rubble, trying to recover his family's bodies so he can give them a proper burial. How will people like that continue?

My heart doesn't have space in it for the flood of emotions I feel. My mind can't contain the faces and stories of all the people I carry with me. It's too much. My heart, my mind, they're on the verge of bursting, ready to explode. Gaza feels so lonely, and so utterly betrayed. And I look at her and I feel so helpless. I wish I could hug her. I wish I could do something – anything – to stop this. I wish I could take all the sadness away.

Usually, hospitals depress me, especially those that are full of displaced or injured people. But today I went to Al-Shifa and, in a lonely corner in the front yard, a man named Nadeem had sourced some posters and paintings, and was inviting children to come draw and colour their thoughts. It was so heartwarming to see children trying to be children. I met a young girl, Layan, who was drawing a house – and then I noticed that most children were drawing houses and Palestinian flags. I think that's what's occupying everyone's minds in Gaza. Having a home of their own, and the dream of a Free Palestine where our flag can wave carefree, without a worry.

Something about the scene around Nadeem was uplifting and heartbreaking at the same time. Metres away, there were martyred and injured people scattered across the yard, yet in front of me there were children drawing and playing with one another.

This is Gaza. This is the Gaza I know.

Day 21 | FRIDAY 27 OCTOBER

I meander through the streets of Gaza, and I can almost hear Her.

How can one feel so much for a city so small? How can a place like this shatter your heart into a million pieces? I love you, Gaza, but I'm angry at you too. I know you are suffering, but we are suffering too, and it feels like you're watching us in silence. Please, Gaza, I beg you – speak to me. Tell me it will get better. Tell me you'll rise again, stronger than before. Lie to me if you must, but say something, anything. Your silence is deafening.

Today, I see an old man walking alone, leaning on his crutch, barely able to move. Mohamed and I rush to help him, but others pass him in the street without a second glance, without seeing him. Blinded by their own worries and fears. This is the first time my resolve in Palestinians shakes, and it's only for a second. Because we're not action heroes. What do you expect people to do?

Cell service is completely unavailable today. Dying people aren't able to call ambulances. I'm supposed to be the eyes of Gaza, to show the world what's happening. But how can I? I'm *in* Gaza and I have no idea what's happening – there's no internet, or cell connection, or fuel, or electricity, or anything!

I love you more than before, Gaza, even as I struggle to recognize you. I'm upset with you, but also for you. Since I was little, mama assured me that things would always get better, and she told me that I shouldn't worry. But now she can't find those words. She can't even lie to me, and tell me that it will be okay.

So, Gaza, I turn to you. At least you – say something!

Day 22 | SATURDAY 28 OCTOBER

Today, I'm thinking of you, Diary. Today, you are in safe hands. I have you and you have me. But tomorrow, you might be under rubble, with nobody to take care of you.

A little boy might find you and scream with happiness: 'A notebook!' To him, you will only be a notebook, and he will be so excited to take you to his tent, and you will go with him and you will burn, and you will make the boy and his family warm for a little time.

If that comes to pass, and your journey is that of a diary that becomes a candle, I just want you to know that you've been a good friend to me.

Day 23 | SUNDAY 29 OCTOBER

It's sometime in the early morning, or sometime late at night. I'd guess between 1 and 2 a.m., but I'm not sure.

I've stopped posting excerpts from my diary on my Instagram page. I always imagined that I'd have more time to be alive. And I want to make sure that if I die, I'll have made some kind of impact. I've always wanted to show the world Gaza through my eyes, so I'm going to publish these excerpts, or at least pass them on to someone to publish for me if I get killed. And I'll include poetry. I'll be like Rupi Kaur.

The idea of leaving a legacy behind is a part of why I've always wanted to be a journalist. In Palestine, there are several writers from modern history who are revered as changemakers because of what they wrote when they were alive. When the sword is as mighty as Israel's, then the pen becomes all the more important. Palestinian writers like Ghassan Kanafani have changed history through their words. It is my dream to be part of that tradition.

I want to write a poem but I can't. It's like a tap has been turned off and nothing comes out. Nothing comes out of nothingness. The poem is a blank page with tears; the poem is the eyes of the people of Gaza. I've tried to describe what I see, but their eyes betray an emotion that I can't put into words.

It's the fear of a grandmother who lived through Al-Nakba, and now worries that worse is happening; it's the desperation of a father who can't provide food and water for his family; it's the guilt of a mother whose arms are no longer a safe place for her kids; it's the resignation of a child who knows what it's like to die of hunger, and it's the innocence of a baby who knows death before life.

Today will be day twenty-three. I think back to day three, when my building was partially demolished, and my family, my neighbours and I all slept in Al-Quds. I thought that was the worst that could happen to me. And then I remember day six, when over a million people were forced to evacuate to the south, and when I believed for the first time that I might die an anonymous girl alone in a hospital, and had a breakdown. Motaz Azaiza and Ameer Abu Aisha calmed me down that day, and reassured me that we'd all be able to evacuate eventually, even though I couldn't stop imagining the worst. I survived, and again thought I'd hit rock bottom.

I eventually came south on day nine, to Khan Younis, where I'm supposed to be safe, but I have not felt safe for a single second since I arrived, even when the rest of my family arrived a couple of days later. And then, two days ago, on day twenty-one, Israel officially cut network service in Gaza, and we found ourselves unable to contact family, friends and even ambulances. Again, I thought, I must be at the nadir of this experience.

But it's day twenty-three and I'm afraid to close my eyes, for fear of reliving the scenes I've seen of children being torn apart, their cries and screams haunting me through the night. My brain is refusing to process the last few days. I don't want to be consigned to history; I don't want to see Gaza demolished. I don't want to see any more people being killed. All I want is a ceasefire. Please, God, let this stop as fast as possible.

It's 8 a.m. now. I barely slept but it's okay. I like to be the first one to wake up and the last one to sleep. That way I can look after everyone, at least during daylight.

I studied the First and Second World Wars at school, and a few years ago Yara gave me a copy of Anne Frank's diary. I thought it was important to know about it for my education, but I considered it a relic of a history that we had left behind us. I never really understood or imagined what the actual experience must have been like, and I never thought I'd ever live through it myself in 2023. Why do we study history when clearly nobody ever learns from it?

I'm blessed that I've survived this long. Humans use stories to understand the world around them and, when the world around them is as hectic as what is around me, there aren't many stories to turn to. But Anne Frank's is one of them, and I cling to that. I wonder if someone will read this one day when their world is falling apart, and they'll empathize with my stories.

Day 24 | MONDAY 30 OCTOBER

I wake up thinking about Mahmoud Darwish. I read his poetic narrative *Why Did You Leave the Horse Alone?* a few years ago, and I'd give anything to read it again now. I want to feel its relatability. I repeat the same lines over and over again in my head:

> 'Why did you leave the horse alone?'
> To keep the house company, my son.
> Houses die when their owners are gone.

And now I wonder how my house feels without us, its owners.

> My house.
> Do you miss me?
> Like I miss you?

Day 25 | TUESDAY 31 OCTOBER

I go to the UNRWA camp in Khan Younis. There are around 33,000 Palestinians living there in terrible conditions. Crowded is an understatement, and no words can really do justice to what I see.

I am roaming around the camp, and I find myself staring into people's eyes again. It has become more than a habit to do this; maybe part of me thinks that if I don't fully understand and absorb these moments, if I don't grasp the maelstrom of emotions in those eyes – the pain and the sadness and the desperation and the resolve and the determination – then I might be hardened by this experience. I'm worried that if I survive it, I might lose my empathy. Their pain is my pain, their determination my determination. They are who I am, and I have to know that and know them to know myself.

Hatem, Mohamed and I are scouting for interviews, when

we come across a tent still being erected. A man is building a part of it while a lady entertains her two adorable babies, and there are three girls giggling nearby. I can tell they are new to the camp. We approach them, introduce ourselves and ask if we can interview the woman. She agrees, and I notice her daughters looking at me and smiling. Once I finish my report, I proceed to the next tent, where an old lady and her son have opened a clay oven to bake for people in exchange for a small amount of money.

Pretty soon, the dad from the first tent approaches me, holding the hands of his beautiful daughters. They want to tell me that they follow me on Instagram and that they love me! I record a video for them and post it.

Eventually the dad mentions a third daughter, Lolo, who wants to come talk to me but is too shy, so I agree to finish up the story with the bakers and return to their tent. Lolo is adorable. She's five years old and, once I break the ice, she is all talk. She shares with me how she has been counting down to her birthday, and how she's made a special calendar to help her. Unfortunately, she had to evacuate her home the day before her birthday, and so she hasn't been able to celebrate it.

Hatem and Mohamed promise her that they'll throw her a party tomorrow, and I argue with them about that – I don't think you should promise kids anything during a Genocide, because you might be killed before you can fulfil it. But they said it, so we go and search for hours for cake. We can't find any (the bakers only did bread), so we just go and buy an assortment of different snacks from the market. We'll go back to Lolo tomorrow, if we survive, and we'll celebrate with her as best as we can.

I can't believe it's day twenty-five. It's been twenty-five days without electricity, without access to clean water and with barely any food or fuel. It's crazy how all we're asking for is a ceasefire, yet all we're getting is body bags. Life was never normal in Gaza, but I miss my life before the Genocide. I miss waking up and going to work. I miss not being able to decide what to wear! Now I literally don't have anything to wear; the black jacket I've had on for the last nineteen days isn't even mine.

I used to be a perfectionist; if I ever wrote a word wrong in my diary, I'd tear the page out and start over. I hated seeing mistakes. I never used to post my writing on social media, because my standards were insanely high. I always had perfect nails; I'd go to a salon multiple times a month to make sure. I always used to work overtime, and go above and beyond, because I couldn't live with the idea that I'd given anything but my best. I used to look on the bright side.

I'm not the same person now and there's nothing perfect about my life. I try to be optimistic, to plan for the time after all this ends, but any control I have has been taken away from me.

Before the Genocide, when I went to sleep, I always used to reflect on how I could be a better version of myself. But now, I just think of other people. My people. I think of all the martyrs and how they all had dreams and a future that they imagined. I think of all the people who have lost their families, and now face a life filled with terrible loneliness. I think of those who are wounded, widowed at hospitals, trying to recover while managing physical and mental trauma. I think of Gaza, and how She became a ghost town in the blink of an eye.

I shift in my sleep, trying to get comfortable. I stare at the ceiling and I think of God.

Day 26 | WEDNESDAY 1 NOVEMBER

I wake up at 10.19 a.m. from the first positive dream I've had in weeks. I don't remember what it was about, but for some reason I'm happy. I hope something good happens today.

Luckily, we weren't killed yesterday, so we surprise Lolo when we get back to the camp and we sing to her even though we don't have any cake or candles or streamers or balloons. And she is so happy. Her smile. It is so contagious, and so genuine that – just for a minute – we forget all about the Genocide, and the pain and the suffering and the loss. Just for one minute.

Lolo and her sisters make me feel like a celebrity, taking pictures with me on multiple phones, just to make sure they don't lose the evidence of my visit. They don't want me to leave, and a part of me wishes I could have stayed there, suspended in that minute, for ever.

On night twenty-six, I sleep, and my dreams are peaceful. Amidst everything happening in Gaza, humans are still humans. In the middle of a powerless existence, I had the power to make at least one family smile and be happy, even if just for a couple of minutes. And in Gaza, where life can be stolen away at a moment's notice, happiness means more. You have to treasure every moment, every laugh and every bit of hope you can. It helps you and those around you to survive.

Day 27 | THURSDAY 2 NOVEMBER

If someone could put their hand inside my heart and just take out all my feelings and put them into words for me, that would be great. But personally, I have no more capacity to try. My dictionary is destitute. My lexicon is levelled. My vocabulary is vacant. And my ability to describe my emotions has deserted me.

I do know that I appear stronger than I am. I feel like there are two versions of me. Day Plestia is optimistic, responsible and powerful. And Night Plestia is me, writing in this diary right now.

I've been wearing the press vest for almost a month now, and it has put a lot of weight on my shoulders. Literally, because it's heavy and it hurts my back, but also figuratively. I feel like I carry a weight of responsibility around with me all the time. I witness and listen to heartbreaking stories every single day, and I never allow myself to break down in front of people. I always try to lift others up. I try to not only be a good listener but to also help.

Day Plestia lives every day as if it's her last, and she acts in the way that I want to be remembered – as someone who brought joy and hope with her. But that's a lot of responsibility, and Night Plestia is constantly terrified that she's not living up to it. Some nights feel like they could be my last more than others, like tonight, and on those nights the thought of how I will spend my final hours keeps me awake.

More than anything, I suppose I'd like to be doing something worthwhile, if possible. I don't want to be killed in my sleep; that seems passive and random, and kind of lame. A better scenario would be to go out while working in the field.

Plestia Alaqad

Day 28 | FRIDAY 3 NOVEMBER

I don't have the energy to write every day. I'm posting less and less on social media because my mental health can't tolerate what's happening any more. My heart aches.

It has been twenty-eight days of literal hell. Gaza has reached a point where it's totally running out of food and clean water. The supermarkets are almost empty; people now spend their days just roaming round, searching for the basic necessities.

We wake up and instead of kids going to school, students to university and adults to work, everyone collectively goes searching for goods that should already be there. It's beyond sad that Gaza has come to this. I remember joking with Mohamed a couple of weeks ago, telling him we'd soon be eating leaves, but more and more that joke is becoming a very literal reality. Even if my family and I can hold off for a bit longer than most, I won't be surprised to see leaf-eating on the streets any time now. Nothing is shocking at this point.

My paternal uncle comes to us devastated, having gotten up early to spend three hours on a fruitless search for eggs. Eggs are a big deal. When you have eggs, you have breakfast, lunch and dinner. So when the Strip runs out of eggs, it makes me more than a little anxious. His brother-in-law arrives shortly afterwards, equally devastated over a lack of tissues.

My uncles bring news of another massacre. It's becoming routine but, deep down, we know we can never get used to it. The sight of blood, the loss of our people — it's all too much to bear. Watching families wander the streets burdened with their belongings, carrying whatever items they were able to salvage from their homes, breaks my heart. Seeing others clutching pillows, unsure of where to go, fills me with a sense of helplessness. I wish I could find the right words to express how I feel, to make sense of it all. But what more can I say or do in the face of such overwhelming tragedy?

Day 29 | SATURDAY 4 NOVEMBER

I am so drained and so tired. I'm sorry for the negativity, but I like to think it's realistic rather than pessimistic. My back hurts from the press vest, and my heart is heavy with emotional exhaustion.

Every day is becoming more dangerous for me as a journalist. Mama is so worried about me, and I understand her, but what can I do about that? What can anyone do to stay safe? There are no safe positions. Even if I become a pickle in a jar, they can steal me.

I might get killed while working, eating or sleeping, I might get targeted any time. But if it's up to me, I'm sticking with the field. The longer I work out there, the surer I am that I'd prefer to die while doing my job. I'm grateful that I have something to offer me a purpose when so many others have had theirs stolen away.

I just hope my family stays safe, and that nothing bad happens to any of my loved ones. I try to be optimistic during the day, especially around kids, but I'm starting to feel that I can't even do that any more. I'll try harder.

Plestia Alaqad

Day 30 | SUNDAY 5 NOVEMBER

It's around 2 a.m., and I'm sitting with my sister Judy, my uncle's wife and my cousin. We're literally silent; everyone is just staring into nothingness. I don't know for sure what's going on inside everyone's head, but I suspect they're all wondering when this nightmare will end.

Let us imagine that a truce is finally announced. Then what? All of these people without homes – where are they supposed to live? All of these people living in schools – where are they supposed to go? And since schools have either been destroyed or are being used as shelters, how will students go back to education? What about all the people seeking refuge in hospitals? What will happen to them?

I don't know who to think of – who deserves my grief? Moms who are unsure of their children's fates, whether they're alive, deceased, injured or lost? The brothers who are missing, or held hostage, with no word about them reaching their families in weeks? The young ones who have been orphaned, left without protection in a world that's consistently telling them their lives aren't worth saving? Can you imagine that there are dead bodies in the street that haven't been buried yet? The scale of the suffering, and the sense of helplessness, is truly unfathomable.

Imagine a street that you travel on every day, with buildings and stores on the left and the right, and neighbours that greet you as you pass by. Now imagine walking down that same street, but all the buildings and stores are gone, and there are no neighbours left to greet you. Instead, all you can hear is a voice crying for help from under the rubble. You turn your back and walk away, because there's nothing you can do to help.

Imagine the pain of that, and you might understand, just for a moment, the pain of the Palestinian people.

A few weeks ago, someone told me that I speak English more than Arabic because I want to hide behind the foreign language, and I didn't understand what he meant. But now, I do understand. Arabic is my first language; I know it not just as a form of communication but as a piece of art. It's lyrical, and volatile, and beautiful, and emotional. Whenever I try to speak about what's happening in Arabic, I break down into tears and I feel angry, because I can express my pain in its purest form. And in Gaza, I don't have time to cry, and I am not afforded the luxury of breaking down. So I prefer to speak in English, to escape my emotions as much as to communicate.

It's 10.30 a.m., I've been awake for an hour and a half, and I've accomplished just about as much as I did in the middle of the night. I've been staring at the ceiling, mostly thinking about how grateful I am to have a ceiling to stare at.

I'm trying to reflect on and understand the past couple of weeks of my life, but I genuinely can't understand. I'm almost twenty-two years old – I'm an adult, and I'm a journalist, but my brain refuses to process what's happening. It leads me to question whether anybody is supposed to understand, whether what's happening is something that a human brain is supposed to comprehend? We are Palestinians. We wake up in our country and we get killed in our country. And nobody seems to notice.

Mohamed, Hatem and I start our day with some essential shopping. We're able to buy some snacks and water, and we even manage to get our hands on a whole box of Indomie noodles – yes, a whole box! Usually, the markets only allow each person to buy a maximum of four packets, but we're allowed a whole box because we're journalists. I feel like a special snowflake, and I take a moment to remember the unmarked joy of my profession.

Then we go searching for toys and colouring books – essentials in a Genocide. Hatem buys a book and some pencils for his son, while Mohamed grabs a few toys for his own children. I myself buy a bracelet kit for my cousins, Bara'a and Reena. Since the beginning of the Genocide, they've been obsessed with making bracelets for everyone. I wish I could say that it was for fun, but they've been branding each bracelet with a name, in case its intended owner gets killed. They want the doctors to be able to identify people. It's sweet, in a sad way. I also buy toy phones for Randa and Lia, two girls displaced at the UNRWA camp in Khan Younis.

Randa and Lia are thrilled with the toy phones, and they squeal in delight when I show them some of the artwork that artists on the internet have been drawing of me and them together. I am full of happiness. You have to take what you can get, and being able to make people happy makes me happy. I'm grateful to be alive, and grateful that I can still make kids smile.

Walking through the camp, I meet a girl I know, Rotana. She's buying socks, and staying here with her family. I'm still not used to randomly running into my friends at camps and in hospitals – it's like they're in the wrong place, displaced in my mind as well as on the ground. Rotana proposes a sleepover;

she says she has sunflower seeds that we can eat all night while we stay up chatting. But here's the thing – I've only ever met Rotana once before this, at a photoshoot. We follow each other on Instagram, but we haven't ever hung out together or anything.

This is my favourite thing about Gaza. It sums up the community of the city, the togetherness and the camaraderie. Rotana doesn't know me, and her family probably doesn't have many resources to share around, but she offers me a place to stay anyway. She has to. It's in our blood.

I eventually decline politely and start to make my way home to my uncle's house. When I get there, I give my cousins the bracelet kits, and they immediately make some for me, Judy and mama. My uncle has five children, Belal, Bader, Bara'a, Reena and Hatem, and they're my joy. They're incredibly loving and caring, and they're almost too proud that their cousin is a well-known journalist. I often end my days with barely any energy, but coming back to them makes everything easier. They're always eager to hear stories about my day, or wanting to play cards together, or begging me to try on my press gear.

Bara'a and Hatem are the youngest, and they never quite settle down. So, a while back, I came up with a game that I think parents and older siblings all around the world have in common: the Quiet Game. And I lure them into playing by offering a reward of candies if they win. It works – they've started coming to me asking to play the Quiet Game, and what sort of older cousin would I be to say no to them? I'd do anything for them, and that decision definitely hasn't got anything to do with my self-interests. Definitely.

Like every night, I go to sleep hoping to wake up to news of a truce. I used to dream of a Free Palestine. Now I just want this to stop.

Day 31 | MONDAY 6 NOVEMBER

Rise and shine.

It's around eight in the morning, and the first thing I do after opening my eyes is open this diary and start writing. I usually write at night, just before I sleep, but I've figured out that people will leave me alone if they see me journaling, so now I do it for a little bit of peace while I wait for Mohamed and Hatem.

Overnight, the cold weather arrived, bringing the wind with it. There was an orchestra outside my window, the sound of the wind battling against the sound of the drones like a cacophony of destruction and violence. Little did the wind know that it wasn't really battling the drones; instead, it was only adding to the burden on us Palestinians. I'm not kidding about the strength of this wind – it's not enough that people can't sleep in their temporary tents because of the relentless drone of the machines above, but now they have to contend with a battering ram at their doors (tent flaps?) trying to kill their children. It leaves them wondering: which will kill us first, the weather or the bombs?

And here I am, inside a house, sleeping on a couch with a blanket covering my tired body. Who am I? Why do I deserve to have a blanket when others don't? I hate how unfair life is, and I'm frustrated that I don't have the capacity to help everyone. I'm just trying my best, and I know it's important to be kind to yourself, but the guilt is real.

Day 32 | TUESDAY 7 NOVEMBER

I think I got about two hours' sleep last night.

I just can't seem to close my eyes and rest. I'm exhausted from the nightmares I keep having – except they're not really nightmares, they're just recollections of the stories of the people I encounter during the daytime, haunting me at night. Sometimes, I wake up and proceed with my day and I see things that are worse than any nightmare. When that happens, I laugh in disbelief, hardly believing that reality has become more terrifying than fantasy.

It has been a month. A month of children, women, men, civilians, doctors, paramedics and journalists getting killed. A month of houses, buildings, hospitals, schools, universities, churches and mosques being demolished. A month of me staring at the ceiling every night before I sleep, wondering when a rocket will come and bring it crashing down on me. A month without clean water, without food, without electricity, without internet, without homes, without family. A month of documenting and reporting how my home, Gaza, is becoming a ghost town.

Every day, every person in Gaza asks themselves: how long until my turn comes around? Every person in Gaza is afraid. How many people need to get killed for the world to finally take action?

Sometimes I wish that I'd just die, for the sake of resting in peace, and sometimes I wish to live, to one day see Palestine become free.

Day 33 | WEDNESDAY 8 NOVEMBER

Did someone remember to check on the pets?

I go to Al-Nasser Hospital today, to report on the people who are displaced there, and I meet an amazing lady. I call her the bird lady. She was displaced together with her daughter and her grandchild, and they're staying in what I can only describe as half a tent, at best. But that's not why she's amazing.

Like most people, she had five minutes to evacuate her house. And in those five minutes, she saved all her pets – a parrot, two tortoises and three other birds. And they're great! We hang out and drink tea, and she even renames one of the tortoises Plestia, in my honour. She's a ray of happiness in an otherwise bleak place.

I am reminded of little Aloos, who wouldn't leave his plant. We all try to take a little bit of home with us, in the hope we can one day return.

Day 34 | THURSDAY 9 NOVEMBER

On an emotional and personal level, today is one of the worst days.

In the morning, I watch as over 50,000 people are forcibly displaced from their homes in North Gaza to camps in the south. It is absolutely harrowing. I stand by as thousands of people file through the safe corridor, their whole lives packed into suitcases in the space of five minutes. It is like a scene out of a dystopian novel – my mind goes straight to the prose in *Nineteen Eighty-Four* – come to life.

And yet there is a kid, Waleed, standing there with sweets,

handing them out to people as they pass him by. He is wearing a cute 'Happy Birthday' hat.

It's weird how a day can be the worst you've experienced, even while retaining sparks of hope. I was so distraught this morning, but in the evening, I visit Randa and Lia, the two little girls who I met at the UNRWA camp ten days earlier. And I just play with them and talk to them for five minutes.

I think this is Gaza. It gives you all kinds of emotions. In the morning, you see people being forcibly removed from their homes and it breaks your heart. And in the evening, you play with two kids for five minutes and it heals something inside of you. It gives you some kind of faith in the sheer persistence of life. If a child can smile, you can do the same, because no matter what the circumstances, humans will stubbornly remain human.

Day 35 | FRIDAY 10 NOVEMBER

I'm the type of person who tries to always search for hope, even in the darkest of times, but lately I've been failing.

Usually, looking at the sky gives me hope. I love watching the clouds, how they form different shapes that every individual interprets in their own unique way. But now, I can't tell the difference between the clouds and the smoke. Hatem and I spend much of the day having a debate about one particular cloud. He was right; it was smoke.

But I enjoy watching sunsets and sunrises, and I do both

today. And nobody can take that away from me, not until they kill me. Not even Israel.

Day 36 | SATURDAY 11 NOVEMBER

I'm so tired of writing that I'm tired, and complaining every day, but what am I supposed to do? Pretend I'm not tired? Fake it till you make it doesn't work during a Genocide. So I'm using this diary to get it out of my system. Deal with it.

Posting on social media, and reporting on what's happening, is becoming more challenging by the day. On an emotional level, the only thing that makes me feel a little bit better is interacting with people, being out in the field, because I can't imagine just sitting back and watching, bearing witness to massacre after massacre. It doesn't last, though. By the time I get home, I'm heartbroken all over again, and I chase sleep that doesn't come to me. My best doesn't feel good enough.

Every night, I wonder if it will be the last of my life. Will there be a tomorrow? I try to look at my family, to gaze at and memorize their faces, just in case.

There is a story that has lived rent-free in my mind for some time. A couple of weeks ago, I went to a hospital and met a five-year-old boy who was the sole survivor of an Israeli attack that killed his entire family. A neighbour had found him, and brought him to the hospital without any identification. He was in a state of shock, unable to speak or respond to questions – he couldn't even say his own name.

The boy wasn't at home when he was attacked. He had been displaced, and his family was staying with three other families at the site that was bombed. It made identifying him almost impossible for the doctors, so they had to rely on the neighbour's knowledge of who had been staying there. Eventually, they wrang out a family name, and reached out to his uncles. But even when they came, they couldn't identify their nephew. His face was too severely injured, his features entirely obscured. They couldn't say if he was theirs. How do you think they felt in that moment?

Last I heard, the doctors were waiting for the boy's injuries to improve so the potential uncles could come and check again. I think he was alone. Maybe he's dead now. I've always thought of death as a negative thing. But now? With everything that's happening? I wonder if it's easier for all these injured kids to pass away in peace, rather than stay alive, hurt and injured, in a collapsed healthcare system destroyed by a ruthless oppressor.

I found a painting of someone's home on a desk in that hospital. Every Gazan is just dreaming of returning to his/her home. (By the way, I don't like using the word Gazan but I have to. I hate how the IOF has divided us by experience – by slaughter. Palestinians in Ramallah or Jerusalem can't relate to those in Gaza, and vice versa. We're all one, but they've managed to make us feel completely separated.)

I miss my home too. I miss sleeping in my bed, I miss fighting with my sister about who will sleep on the couch, I miss making lunch in the kitchen and I miss the sleepovers I used to have with my friends in my house. I miss everything.

Day 37 | SUNDAY 12 NOVEMBER

I've run out of words to describe my feelings, or what's happening.

That's all I want to say today.

Day 38 | MONDAY 13 NOVEMBER

Mohamed, Hatem and I often like to pass the time speculating on how we'll die. I've always thought that I'll die in a car accident, but now I'm not so sure.

Today, I tell them that if they see me targeted, see me become injured with burns and amputations, to please refrain from saving my life. I've thought about it a lot, and I don't want to live without a hand or a leg. Mohamed says he'd be fine without a leg. Hatem pauses, and says he needs time to come up with his answer. He never comes up with one.

The perfect victim. That's what the world expects Palestinians to be. Over the years, the world has passively watched as we've been killed, displaced and stripped of our basic rights.

This ongoing tragedy has conditioned people to believe that our primary role is to be those who suffer and die at the hands of Israel. This normalization of violence against us has resulted in our dehumanization in the eyes of the world. We are no longer seen as individuals with dreams, families and futures, but as mere statistics in an endless cycle of oppression. Killing us has become an accepted norm, and our existence is reduced to a narrative of suffering: suffering which results in death or survival.

However, this superficial perception fails to account for the aftermath of such survival. The physical and emotional scars, the displacement, the loss of loved ones, and the constant fear and uncertainty remain unacknowledged. Surviving is not synonymous with living – it's a continuing battle against trauma and despair.

The world's expectation of passive victimhood denies us our agency and humanity. It overlooks our resilience, our resistance and our desires for dignity and justice. This skewed perception must be challenged.

Palestinians are not just victims. We are people, human beings with hopes, aspirations and the right to enjoy a peaceful and dignified life. The world must recognize our struggle not just as victims of senseless violence but as individuals fighting for our rightful place.

Day 39 | TUESDAY 14 NOVEMBER

It rains today. Rain usually gives me hope, but today all I can think about are all the displaced people of Gaza, and how they might manage. I hope we survive this winter.

I've been trying to film a video update all day, but I just continue to stare blankly at my camera. I'm sick of repeating the same sentence again and again, reporting that the situation is just getting worse.

It's getting really crowded here in the south. The markets and shops are literally empty, to the point that it becomes an achievement if you're able to find anything to buy. And there are still people in the north that can't evacuate, because someone is injured or because they have too many kids or because elderly people can't walk or one of a hundred other reasons. Migrating from the north isn't easy – and even when you get here, the reward isn't worth it.

Hatem does manage to capture one bright spot. He is there to film as two kids, probably four or five years old, throw caution to the wind and dance in the rain. It is a beautiful, reckless scene – full of freedom. I love how children can find hope and joy, even in the darkest of times, just from the rain.

Day 40 | WEDNESDAY 15 NOVEMBER

I only sleep for a few hours every day. What trauma will greet me today?

It's a dad in a hospital. His name is Adam, and he tells me about something his five-year-old daughter said to him as she came to after an attack on their home. 'Did everyone go to sleep and wake up without a hand, like me?' she asked him.

Imagine being only five years old, and instead of fantasies about games or clothes or *joy*, having those thoughts in your mind. I find myself thinking more about Adam than his daughter, though. How do you think he manages to sleep, knowing what preoccupies his child's mind? I can only pray that God grants them strength for now, and survival eventually.

I remember being sixteen years old, browsing Tumblr. I was obsessed with quotes that promised 'this too shall pass' or that 'every storm creates a rainbow'. But do you think those quotes apply in a Genocide, or are they really only true for First World problems? I look forward to meeting the adult versions of all these amputee and wounded children when they're all grown up. I hope they heal – even though I believe that there are some things that we never heal from, but we just have to learn how to cope with.

Day 41 | THURSDAY 16 NOVEMBER

Lately, I've been obsessed with checking the time. I want it to pass quicker, but it's not cooperating. Everything moves so slowly.

It's around 10 p.m. and I'm reflecting on the last forty days.

My heart is so heavy. I want to cry, but I know that if I start, I won't stop. I'm not a tough person, and I'm not trying to put up some kind of brave front by restraining myself. It's just that I need personal space to cry, and I don't have any. So even crying has become a privilege now.

I went to Shuhada Al-Aqsa Hospital again today. I wish I had the capability to report on every single story, every single person I meet, but I don't have the time or equipment, let alone the battery power or internet connection to upload everything. The reality is I have to choose which stories are worth reporting on, like some sort of sick judge of human suffering. Another layer of trauma for a journalist in Gaza.

What's sad is that people have become reluctant to talk to the media, because they feel that it's useless. And can I blame them? Can I promise them that sharing their story, reliving their trauma, will change anything in the world? No. All I can tell them is that I'll try to do them justice, and that's not enough for people who are dying.

I think people in Gaza are divided into two groups. The first is made up of those who, out of dignity, want to share their stories with the world – to prove what's happening is happening, so their experiences aren't for nothing. The second group are those who, also out of dignity, don't want to share their stories with the world – because they don't want to be seen as displaced and hungry. Both groups are proud in very different ways, and I don't mind either. But the second group is growing. Now nobody wants to talk at all.

The hospitals in Gaza are full of amputee kids. They're the saddest stories by far. A week ago, I met a baby girl, Fatma – my grandmother's name. Fatma had lost both of her legs. I spoke to her mother, and she just kept repeating how she wished that it was her legs that had been amputated instead of her daughter's. She told me that Fatma had come as a blessing after fourteen years of infertility. And I just stood there beside her, blankly reporting on the scene, privately wishing that I could somehow alleviate her and Fatma's pain.

I met a girl today called Bilsan. She's maybe ten years old. She has dreams of being a teacher, but right now she's stuck at the hospital, limbless and with scars all over her beautiful face. What did she *do*? What did she do to deserve that?

Despite her tragic circumstances, there's still joy in Bilsan. When her dad spoke to me about her, about how she's the smartest in her class, and how she gathers all her neighbours' kids to teach them in her yard after school, her eyes shone with pride. An educator at heart, I told him! He smiled, and said how it was fortunate that Israel had targeted their house at night rather than in the morning, because at least Bilsan's students weren't there. So maybe the greater massacre was avoided.

I hope Bilsan holds on to her passions. I hope she follows her dreams and grows up to be the teacher she wants to be. I hope she lives, and I hope that she has the chance to pursue whatever path her heart chooses. I hope and I hope and I hope.

I wonder how many Bilsans there are out there. How many stories that remain untold.

Day 42 | FRIDAY 17 NOVEMBER

I often ask kids what they miss most from their lives before 7 October. The answers are usually typically innocent: *my friends, my school, my house.* But today I'm asking myself this question, and I don't have an answer. I don't want to choose just one thing to miss. I miss everything. Literally everything.

I miss being able to sleep.

I miss sleeping in my bed.

I miss waking up in my bed.

I miss my morning routine, and my night-time routine.

I miss having a closet full of clothes and complaining about having nothing to wear.

I even miss my diary.

The original one, not this ugly notebook.

Though still one that I was grateful to find.

I miss having tea with mama, and I miss taking that time for granted.

I miss fighting with my sister over who gets to take a shower first.

I miss Dana.

I miss watching kids play.

I miss my house.

I miss my life.

I miss my Gaza.

I miss a life that's only a memory now.

Most of all, I miss feeling safe.

Sometimes it feels like I'll never feel safe again.

It's funny how a Genocide changes a person. If I'd written the above before 7 October, I would have bullied myself. 'What are you, a wannabe poet?' But because Genocide Plestia wrote it, it's perfect. How can you fake anything in the middle of this?

Day 43 | SATURDAY 18 NOVEMBER

My friends and I used to debate whether a person can truly give something they don't have. I don't think there's a debate any more. The people of Gaza need more hope than anybody, yet they give it to me in abundance. I can now confidently assert that the person who needs something the most is the one who most freely gives it.

There have been days where I've been on the edge of breaking down, only for a little kid to give me a cup of water or a piece of candy, restoring my faith in life and making me feel like it's worth living again. If that kid can live in a world where everything has been stolen from them, and still display kindness and compassion, then so can I.

My friend Ali has been killed by the Israelis. I saw it on Instagram earlier today. He was so much more than a waiter at Bellini, the restaurant I so often frequented before the

Genocide. He was everyone's friend. He knew each customer's order by heart, and his smile would light up the whole room. I've known Ali for over ten years. Even as the restaurant moved locations, he remained, a constant presence. When I went to Cyprus for three years, I came back and Ali was still there waiting for me. He was like a landmark in Gaza, a beloved figure cherished by all.

The only solace in the news of his passing is the outpouring of stories that have emerged, celebrating his life. All Gazans knew and loved Ali, and it feels like we're all collectively mourning his loss. The communal grief feels like a comforting embrace. It reminds me of how small this city is, how tight-knit our community. It's amazing the strength of the love that can come from such a small place.

The world sometimes treats us like terrorists, trying to justify its complacency in allowing us to be massacred. And we know the perception, we read the propaganda just like everyone else. But the reality is that we're the opposite.

In Gaza, you are never just a number. Even though we lose more people than our hearts can handle, every single one is remembered, and loved, and mourned. Because that's what you'd want to happen for you, and that's the least that a human deserves.

Day 44 | SUNDAY 19 NOVEMBER

Today is another sad day. We've run out of fuel, so we can't go anywhere to do our jobs. Being a journalist is already challenging, but Israel somehow manages to make our job even harder.

Even though this is my extended family's house, I'm starting to get really disturbed by the fact that it's not mine. I need my space back. I feel like I'm being choked, and not being able to go outside is making it so much worse.

What am I supposed to do today? Just stare at the sadness in everyone's eyes around me? Or cry all the tears I haven't cried – but noiselessly, remember, so as not to disturb the steady thrum of the drones? I just want to scream all of my emotions out, but that's a privilege that I can't afford.

At least I'm getting a glimpse of what everyone else does in a Genocide. My teta prays for most of the day. She splits her time between reading the Qur'an and staring wordlessly into space. I can tell she's thinking about her house, and that she misses her TV. What did your grandmother do today?

My mom is reading to pass the time – *Forty* by Ahmed Al-Shugairi – but I don't think she's getting much enjoyment out of it. She does the laundry at some point. I remember how I used to see my mom, at work in her office as the head of middle school at the American International School. Now, she's displaced in Khan Younis, at her in-laws' house, sitting on the balcony with nothing but a round blue wash basin to keep her company. I offer to help her but she declines.

My sister is actually doing something – she's helping my aunt bake bread – which is a revelation in and of itself. I think she's mainly there for the chat, though.

As for me, I'm still trying to process how unpredictable life is. This time last year, I was chilling at my house in Gaza City, living that post-graduate life where half your time is spent trying to figure your life out, and the other half is spent watching TV and hanging out with other post-graduates who pretend like half their time isn't spent watching TV. And now? Here I am. Displaced.

There are approximately eight billion people in the world, I think. I can't check, I don't have internet access. Each of them is experiencing today in a unique way. I wonder about the woman complaining about her job, or the little boy complaining to his mother about having to go to school. How would they feel if they got a glimpse into Gaza? It's interesting to think how the life that one person hates can be another's dream.

I'm going to try to sleep, and hope that Mohamed finds us some fuel so we can work tomorrow. He mentioned bicycles the other day. But how am I supposed to ride around on a bike while wearing the vest and helmet, two items that at this stage I'm fairly confident are made of the same material as Thor's hammer?!

Day 45 | MONDAY 20 NOVEMBER

Maybe I should kill myself before the IOF target me and kill me themselves.

I'm not a suicidal person, and I've never said that out loud – I don't think I ever will. But everything that's happening is making me lose my mind.

Sometimes I consider the idea that being killed for Palestine might be an honour. Other times, I worry that I'll be targeted and somehow survive, but in pieces. I imagine that a leg or a hand will be buried, and the rest of my body will remain alive. But that thought hurts, so I try to avoid it, especially before I sleep.

Belal Jadallah was killed by the IOF yesterday, and I'm still in denial. He meant a lot to me, on a personal and a professional level. Before the Genocide, when I was doing internships and workshops at Press House Palestine, Belal was my mentor, the first person I'd tell about any kind of success, and the first person I'd go to for advice.

I've always thought of journalism as a noble profession, but I never knew that being a Palestinian journalist is a crime. When I see news of a journalist being killed, or a journalist's family being targeted, I wonder if my family will be next. Nowadays, mama tells me to leave my press vest in the car with Mohamed and Hatem, not to bring it home, because she is afraid that the vest and helmet will draw attention. I understand her fear, obviously. But it bothers me that this is the world we're living in. My whole life, I dreamed of wearing the press outfit, and now I have to hide it. As if I'm a criminal, concealing the evidence of her crime. Except my only crime is existing.

It makes sense that Israel would target Belal, but I think my brain had put him in a place in my head where he'd always be there to turn to, and now he's not. I don't want to write about him in the past tense. I don't want to say 'was' instead of 'is'. He's gone, and I don't want him to be.

I was so excited for the end of the Genocide, to go to Press House and show him all my work, all my accomplishments. I think he would have been proud of me. What's the point of wearing a safety helmet and press vest? I don't want to wear them any more; they're like giant targets instead of safety nets. Israel is targeting journalists. And doctors. And lawyers. And engineers. Basically, anybody who might practically be able to help rebuild Gaza in the future.

How long until they get to me?

The Last Night in Gaza

The news comes so suddenly.

My mom calls me at around 7 p.m., while I am at Hamad Hospital in Khan Younis, to tell me that we're going to leave tomorrow, first thing in the morning. I have less than twenty-four hours' notice.

It's a sad reality that the borders aren't open for everyone to travel through, and a sadder reality that the reason we are travelling is so that we don't get killed, or starve to death, or be subjected to further forced displacement.

To pass through the borders, you either have to pay a huge amount of money, be lucky enough to have dual citizenship or have family members abroad who can get you out of Gaza – which is the case for us. My uncle happens to be Palestinian/ Australian, so he's able to apply for emergency humanitarian visas for us through the Australian Home Office, and we're able to leave.

Mohamed and Hatem are with me when I receive the news. It isn't a happy moment, or one of relief. We are all sad. They try to convince me to stay, as if I have an option. Then we realize that we've forgotten to eat all day, and that all we have to hand are candy bracelets. They make up our last meal together.

I go to the hospital's courtyard to say goodbye to the bird lady, but I can't find her tent. Her neighbours (can you say neighbours in a displacement camp?) tell me that she was forced to take her tent down because of the strength of the wind. I think she has found another tent to stay in, with another family, but I don't have time to check.

Mohamed and Hatem drive me back to my family's house. This is the saddest ride of my life, knowing that it is the last time we'll ever work together, as a team, in that car.

That car is our home. It's where we eat, where we've slept, where we charge our phones, store our belongings and spend most of our time. How can a hunk of metal with four doors become a home to three people?

When I arrive at the house, I go upstairs to my uncle's flat and tell him and my cousins that I am leaving in a couple of hours. I can see that my cousins are happy for me, that I am going to make it out alive, but they are clearly sad to be left behind.

We try to make the most out of our last hours together. We share stories, memories of times gone by, when we were younger and the world hadn't fallen apart. My cousin Belal sings for us, and Amani makes us cappuccinos to drink (coffee is rare – I searched for hours to find it, so we were saving it for a special occasion). We keep trying to distract ourselves from the future, from the fact that me and my family would be leaving Gaza a couple of hours later.

I barely sleep.

The Last Morning in Gaza

My entire extended family, all the cousins, wake up early to see us off. Bara'a is crying up until the last minute. I tell her that this is a 'see you later', not a for ever goodbye.

Mohamed and Hatem pick us up – me, Judy, mama and teta – and drive us to the Rafah border. The entire journey, teta looks out the window, shocked by how crowded and overwhelmed Gaza is. She can't believe that the main mode of transportation has become carts with donkeys rather than cars.

Mohamed and Hatem stay with us at the crossing point, waiting with us for hours before our names are called to get on a bus that will take us to the Palestinian side of the crossing. Saying goodbye to my colleagues is the hardest part. Over the last month and a half, I've seen Mohamed and Hatem more than I've seen my family – and they've become more than family to me. I've learned so much from them.

We have the kind of relationship where we can understand each other without even having to speak. I hope we get to work together again. I hope that instead of reporting on a Genocide and the forced displacement of our people, we get to report on the beauty of Gaza. I don't want to see more people getting killed. I don't want to see my Gaza more demolished than it already is.

I've been working with Mohamed and Hatem for the last forty-five days, almost 24/7. We lived in the same car together, knowing that our fates were connected. If we died, we died together. And if we survived, we survived together. Leaving on my own, making it out alive alone, feels like a betrayal, even if nobody but me thinks of it that way. I just hope this Genocide ends soon.

Life is unpredictable. One day, you can be chilling at your house, and the next day you can find yourself displaced in a hospital – the first of many displacements. Then, one day, you can find yourself forcibly displaced out of your own country. Who knows what's next in this journey? How far will life take me?

When the 2021 Israeli Aggression started, I was glad that I was in Gaza, with my friends and family. This time, I'm leaving. And that is the difference between an Aggression and a Genocide.

My body may be leaving Gaza, but my heart is still there.

Leaving Gaza Alone

Gaza, will you long for me?
As I long for you?
Will you await my return?
Will your streets still be there to greet me?
Will the woman with the birds still be there when I come back?
Will Randa and Lia remember me?
Will the sea notice my absence?
The idea of me holding on to you,
While you move on without me,
Terrifies me.
I left Gaza today.

The Aftermath

The world is big, yet there's no space for me in it.

After Gaza | NOVEMBER 2023

I'm in Egypt right now, and there are only stars in the sky. I haven't heard the sound of bombs for a couple of hours. I'm not used to it. I'm looking up, but all I see are stars – no drones or quadcopters. I'm in a fancy hotel room, full of different lighting options, and it has two comfy beds and even a bathroom with a bathtub and hot water. I feel so privileged. Too privileged. So privileged that I decide not to shower; I just sleep on the clean sheets in the dirty clothes that I've been wearing all along. Plestia, before the Genocide, would have judged me so harshly right now.

How can there exist a whole other life, just a few kilometres away in Gaza?

I go shopping today, and for the first time in my life, it feels like a mission instead of an activity that I enjoy. I hate how everything feels pointless but everything is. I'm usually picky when it comes to buying clothes, but today I just go for anything because I have literally nothing to wear. I think about how fortunate I am to be able to buy a jacket, while my friends back home are probably freezing right now.

And you know what really annoys me? The fact that I feel blessed and privileged to have slept on a bed last night and to have bought a jacket today. Should my standards be that low just because I'm a Palestinian?

Remember how I used to tell you that I kept bumping into friends and family in Gaza because everyone was displaced at the same time? The same thing is happening here. In the mall in Cairo today, I see several people I know from Gaza. It doesn't fill me with any kind of relief. It makes me sad that we're all being forced to leave our home just to seek safety.

Lots of people recognize me from the news, and from my social media platforms, and approach me to say hi and take pictures. They express their appreciation for me and my work, saying they feel like they already know me, almost as if we are friends. They say many kind things, I suppose, but I am just physically standing there, smiling without really listening. My mind is elsewhere.

Obviously, I appreciate people's love and support. But I don't view myself the same way people view me. I don't see myself as a heroine. I feel like what I did was nothing compared to what was happening on the ground. I probably documented less than ten per cent of the struggles people in Gaza are going through.

Physically, I'm in Egypt, but mentally I'm in Gaza. I just keep wondering how many more Palestinians have to get killed for this to end? How much more of Gaza needs to be demolished for Israel to say 'enough'? I feel so naive. Every night, I tell myself that things can't get worse, only for the next day to prove me wrong. My heart aches with a pain that words cannot fully describe.

Life will never be the same again. Since 7 October, my view of the world has been irreversibly altered.

I will never be the same Plestia that I was before.

After Gaza | DECEMBER 2023

I once read a book called *In December All Dreams Come to an End.* I don't remember what it's about, and usually I don't like books with pessimistic titles, but I do remember that I decided to read it because December is my favourite month. I feel like there's happiness in the air in December. So I was intrigued to read about someone who dislikes it. Is that even possible?

For me, December is a reminder of how far you've come in life in any given year. Even if you don't like your life, or you're not proud of the version of yourself that you've been, December offers you the opportunity to let go of all the things that are bothering you, and to start again. It's a month of vision boards, of dreaming and manifesting. Also, the cold weather gives you an excuse to be lazy, and to stay in bed drinking hot chocolate and watching movies. What more can you wish for?

I remember one day in December, in middle school, when the weather got so cold in Gaza City that the school gave us the day off. And it was my birthday! It was the best day of my life. Growing up, I always used to celebrate Christmas with Yara and her family. I'd go over to her house after school, we'd order fast food – usually pizza from Al-Taboon – and decorate the tree and house in whatever way we wanted, taking frequent breaks to dance to 'Y.M.C.A.', of course.

December has always treated me well. Until this year.

This year, houses where people had enjoyed the cosiness of the season have turned into cold tents full of scraps of their possessions. The people who are supposed to be dreaming, manifesting new beginnings, are getting killed. Christians who would be celebrating Christmas, like Yara and her family, now find themselves trapped in the churches that should be lit up with lights and joy and song. The sounds of fireworks and celebration have turned into the sounds of airstrikes and bombs. The fathers who would be holding bags full of gifts for their children are instead holding bags full of their children's limbs. The happiness in the air, this December, has become sadness and grief.

And now I understand how, in December, all dreams can come to an end. How can Palestinians dream of a new year, of new beginnings, when they don't know that they'll survive from one minute to the next?

Yet – as delusional as having hope may sound, I will try not to let hopelessness get the best of me. I don't have control over my life right now; I don't have the luxury of making any decisions for myself. I don't have any options. But what I do have control over is my spirit. And so, my only New Year's resolution for this year is to not allow anyone, not even the Israeli occupation, to kill my spirit.

Today is my birthday. My favourite day of the year.

Generally, I love birthdays and celebrating people. Specifically, I love *my* birthday. I feel like I'm the centre of the universe on my birthday, that the whole world revolves around me! But this year it's different. I'm distant from happiness. I don't feel seen, or that I've been treated like a human.

It's ironic that 10 December is also Human Rights Day, the day that the Universal Declaration of Human Rights was proclaimed by the United Nations General Assembly in Paris back in 1948. It's the most translated document in the world, setting out the fundamental human rights that we have universally agreed should apply to every human being on earth. Unless they're Palestinian, it seems.

I turned twenty-two today, but I feel so much older for the experiences that I've been through. They've aged me. Today feels less like my birthday, and more like a day to remind me that I have no rights in this world other than the right to eventually expire.

If I'm grateful for anything, though, it's that the best-case scenario (within a worst-case scenario) happened. My family and I are safe, and we've made it out alive. My twenty-second birthday wish is for a Free Palestine.

After Gaza | JANUARY 2024

Today is 5 January 2024.

Yes, you read the date right. We're in 2024 now, and the Genocide is still ongoing. You'd think that things would be getting better, but no – it's only getting worse, and the death toll is increasing. I check the news every day, hoping I'll find anything other than Israel killing and starving and forcibly displacing Palestinians, but I don't. There isn't anything.

So I watch videos of my homeland being erased. And I'm heartbroken because I can no longer recognize the places and neighbourhoods of Gaza, and heartbroken is an understatement. My rational brain tells me that we can't have reached the worst point yet, because we never have, but I can't imagine how it can get any worse.

It's around eleven in the morning. I wake up, I brush my teeth, I wash my face and I head to the kitchen to make a cup of tea. Then I open my laptop and start working. It feels like as normal a morning as I can have, until I see a tweet from my friend Heba:

> I miss waking up in the morning and making a mug of coffee and using my laptop. As simple as that.

I keep thinking about how privileged I am now that I have shelter, water to wash my face and a kitchen in which to make a cup of tea to start my day. What kind of world do we live in where drinking a cup of coffee and using a laptop is a person's dream?

My cup of tea remains untouched, staring at me as I stare back at it.

I'm aware that I've been writing less lately. It's because I don't feel like it. I don't feel like doing anything, really. I spend half my day staring at the ceiling until I fall asleep, and the other half trying to catch up with the friends I have that are still alive.

I have nothing interesting to tell you.

After Gaza | FEBRUARY 2024

I rarely go back and read through my writing, but I do often think about how our version of a memory changes each time we recollect it. How a memory, in our minds, might not reflect an accurate picture of what happened. I think that's why I love my diary so much; it helps me to document and remember things accurately, and it's a place I can revisit if I ever want to relive a memory. There's something terribly and beautifully honest about the urgency and immediacy of writing something down that you know you can't change.

I miss Gaza's sea. I used to spend so much of my time in Q cafe, beside the sea. It felt like home. Today, the news reaches me that it has been destroyed, bombed by the IOF in yet another casual display of destruction. I'm devastated – not so much for the building itself, but for the idea that Israel is systematically killing all of our most treasured memories, leaving nothing behind for us to find comfort in.

I can't put into words how much I hate my life right now. I don't even feel that I can call it a life. It feels like I'm watching other people's lives from the sidelines, without participating in them myself. I'm just watching how everyone is going on with their days while I'm trapped inside my own head. I just want to feel happy, like genuinely happy, not happy in a deluded way over the fact that I was finally working as a journalist, all the while pretending to forget that I was reporting on the Genocide of my own people.

Right now, this sadness feels like it will last for ever. I keep telling myself that nothing is for ever, and that it will pass, and that I'll be able to be happy again. But right now, that feels so far away.

Plestia Alaqad

I learn, from an Instagram story, that the IOF have killed my friend Shima.

I never thought I'd learn about her death through social media – not that I ever thought I'd have to say goodbye to her this early in our lives. I am scrolling through stories, and a mutual connection has posted her picture with the caption 'may her soul rest in peace'. I read the words again, trying to understand them. Is Shima gone for ever?

I met Shima when we were both in tenth grade. She was that quiet person in the classroom; the one who only spoke when there was something (usually smart) to say. We used to see each other a lot – we took a two-year English course together – so we became really close. She even invited me to her birthday party; I remember going to her house, celebrating with her friends and family.

We bonded over a love of reading and writing; we used to exchange books with each other, leaving sticky notes on the parts we most enjoyed because we didn't want to ruin the text with highlighters. The last book we exchanged was called *Think Big*; I don't even remember what it's about, but I remember how much I enjoyed having a friend to share my passion for literacy with.

I hate that I'm here and she's not. What hurts me most is that I don't remember the last time I talked to her. I thought we'd have forever ahead of us, and that we'd be able to hang out any time we wanted. Because that future was assured, I was content to keep our relationship at a level where I would react to her social media stories – to know that she was happy and alive was more than enough for me.

I always thought we'd have more time. But the truth is we didn't, and we never will again, and that will stay true for all my relationships as long as Israel continues its occupation of Palestine. And now I've learned that lesson the hard way.

I know, deep down, that she's in a better place now.

I'd very much like to understand why December me thought that making it out alive would be the best-case scenario. Because right now? I can't see it. I'm safe and alive, but I don't think I know what being alive truly means. I've always struggled comprehending death – how someone's consciousness can be present one minute and gone the next – but lately I've been struggling to comprehend being alive. How can someone be in the middle of so many people and still feel like they're nowhere?

In Gaza, everyone has their own identity. We are doctors, journalists, businessmen. But outside of Gaza, who are we? We become just another statistic: refugee number 120, next please. In Gaza, everyone has a home, but outside, we're just unwanted tourists. Or should I say 'refugees'?

We live in a world where to be Palestinian and to be alive is a luxury. Where you need to be an amputee to be deserving of empathy, as if it's an affliction that should draw pity and not outrage. As a Palestinian, you're only expected to be seen crying, and displaced. You're Palestinian – you can't be human. You can't have any other hobbies or interests outside of being a victim. A perfect victim to fit the world's standards for what you're worth.

The world is so used to us being killed and tortured by Israel that it has forgotten that at the end of the day we are humans who want nothing more than to live normal lives, safe in our homeland.

After Gaza | MARCH 2024

Days are passing by, and I'm surviving, not living.

I'm now in Australia, sitting in the sunroom of Khalo Tareq's house. Of all the places in the world, I never imagined that I'd end up here, in a country that I know nothing about, apart from the fact that it has kangaroos and spiders. Growing up, I don't remember watching any news on the TV about Australia.

Khalo has two kids who are so excited that their cousins are finally visiting them in Australia. The whole time, they've been asking us about what places we want to visit, what food we're interested in trying and telling us about their favourite places that they want to take us to. It's sweet, honestly – but all I want to do is sleep, click a button and turn off all my thoughts and emotions until further notice. In their defence, they buy me a T-shirt with 'FIVE MORE MINUTES' written on it, as a tribute to my mumblings early in the morning.

At their encouragement, our first destination in Australia is the zoo. You can imagine how I feel about going somewhere to see animals trapped in cages. But I go anyway, because I care about my family and getting to know my cousins, and I can see how excited they are at the prospect.

While we are at the zoo, a temporary ceasefire is announced in the Gaza Strip. While that might sound like good news, it's not. The killing of Palestinians is just on pause for a couple of days, like a video game. And during that time, Palestinians will learn about the deaths of their friends and families, they'll be digging through the rubble to try to recover their bodies and visiting their bombed-out homes. While I'm at the zoo.

I'm sure there's more to Australia than kangaroos and spiders. But right now, I once again feel like I'm living in two separate worlds. One Plestia is in a zoo in suburban Melbourne, but the other is in a shelled-out building in Gaza, alongside my people. I feel trapped; I dislike the outlook of both worlds that I'm in. I hope these feelings are only temporary.

I know the feeling of homesickness. I used to feel it from time to time when I was studying in Cyprus, far away from home. But now the homesickness is different.

I'm homesick for a home that no longer exists.

Every day that passes while my people and I still suffer is a heavy day, but some days are heavier than others.

Today is International Women's Day, and I'm questioning the point of it. Is it even international? On this day, when people are celebrating and honouring women all around the world, there are thousands upon thousands of women being killed, starved, displaced and tortured in every way possible in Gaza.

Today, I'm thinking of all the young girls who have been forced to grow into women too early, and of all the ones who never even got that chance. All the mothers who have experienced incomparable loss, and all the pregnant women who are struggling to find food and take care of themselves. I'm thinking of the trauma that every woman in my family has suffered for generations now, of how my teta was displaced from Jaffa when she was only two years old.

And I think of mama and what she's had to go through. She was born and raised in Kuwait. She went to Jordan for university, where she married my dad. After moving first to Iraq for seven years, and then to Pakistan for her master's degree, she settled in Gaza in her thirties. She has been there for twenty years. Now, she's in her fifties, and because of the Genocide, she has been forced to move again, to Australia. It feels like if you're Palestinian, or even married to one, your life is a series of endless displacements.

All I can do is pray for things to get better and try to hold on to a string of hope.

I scroll through my phone, feeling bored, when I receive a notification from Dana.

You should see my face, and how happy I am. For a moment, I don't want to open the message, or read it, just because I want to have a notification with her name on my screen. Dana's my second sister. We normally share every single detail of our lives with one another, and it's been so difficult to be so far away from her not knowing anything about her life.

I remember once in 2021, mama and Judy went to Egypt for a couple of weeks and Dana and her sister Rafaa stayed over at our house the whole time. It was one of the best times of my life. We would cook together, order food whenever we wanted, go out together and then come back and have a sleepover.

I can't put into words how much I love Dana, and how much our friendship means to me. It's so hard for me that I can't now talk to her on a daily basis, that I'm unable to even hear her voice. She only texts me when she can, which is every two weeks or so, and one time she didn't text me for a whole month because of the internet situation.

Life is already difficult, and right now it's even harder because I don't have Dana to talk to. At least she's still alive. But I hate how I live in a world where I'm supposed to be happy and grateful because my best friend is alive.

I wanted to spend today answering the backlog of messages on my WhatsApp, and checking up on my friends, but I don't. Instead, I end up just going through the profiles of my friends and family, staring at their pictures. Nobody in Gaza looks the same as they did before; everyone is thinner and sadder.

I've known my classmate Salma since we were children. Her profile picture is of her and her parents at her university graduation – I was there and I took that picture. I captured how proud her parents were and how happy she was that her family were there for her on her big day. Now? Salma is stuck abroad, doing a master's degree. Her parents are in Gaza, and she's mentally there with them.

Nour was my colleague at Press House Palestine. But Press House Palestine doesn't exist any more; it was destroyed. Her profile picture is of her house, bombed.

My friend Yara has a profile picture of her and her nephew, Maher, playing together in the garden of her house. The picture is so genuine, so full of emotion – they both look so happy together. But now, Maher is no longer an innocent three-year-old. He has aged and changed a lot over the last six months. How could he not, given everything he has seen? In Gaza, children aren't allowed to be children. Maher turned four during the Genocide; he spent his birthday trapped in a church.

I keep scrolling through my WhatsApp. My friends who don't live in Gaza still look the same, they're still happy. There isn't any sadness in their eyes, they haven't lost any weight, the places in their profile pictures still exist and their group shots aren't missing anyone.

I don't envy them, I'm glad there are people on this planet that are safe and happy. But I cannot understand how the worth of your life can be determined by where you're from. Why is it that Palestinians are so dehumanized that the world believes it's our God-given *role* to die? If what is happening in Gaza was happening in any other country, would the world remain as silent and calm?

Ameer Abu Aisha was shot today, killed by a sniper. He was a rock, managing to keep calm in his role with the Red Crescent Society even as his family were being killed and his staff were becoming overwhelmed. And he still found time to help and support me, as well as everybody else who asked for his attention. We have lost so many incredible souls to this Genocide, to the brutality of the Israeli regime. May he rest in peace.

The Eyes of Gaza

Leaving Gaza was, without a doubt, the hardest decision I've ever had to make, and I didn't have much time to make it. I kept asking myself which guilt I could live with: the survivor's guilt of leaving Gaza, or the survivor's guilt of my loved ones getting killed while I remained alive? I don't wish for anyone to ever be put in a position where they have to choose between staying in their homeland and staying alive.

The sad reality is that everyone in Gaza experiences survivor's guilt in one way or another. A Palestinian mourns the loss of a family member, only to feel even more sorrow knowing that another family has lost all its members but one sole survivor. That survivor, in turn, feels grief compounded by the realization that there are families that can't even bury their loved ones, as they remain trapped under rubble. It's an endless cycle.

You know what's funny? How ironic life is. I receive messages from strangers all over the world about how they feel survivor's guilt because they're able to eat, sleep, play with their kids or go to school. This has led me to realize that we all feel survivor's guilt, whether we're Palestinians or not. The irony is that we're all victims of this world. So, if we should feel anything, we should feel sorry for ourselves.

How devastating is it that we live in a world where the killing of babies and children is allowed just because they're Palestinian? And protesting and saying this is wrong might get you suspended from work or school just because it hurts the emotions of the killer. Have we become so dehumanized that killing has become justified and normalized?

You might be wondering what to do to not feel survivor's guilt or sorry for yourself. The answer is that we should keep speaking up for Palestine, even if that doesn't change the world. We must not allow the world, as cruel as it might seem, to change our hearts. It's important that at the end of the day, when you look at yourself in the mirror, you see a person who stands up for what's right in this world.

After Gaza | APRIL 2024

I'm reading a book by Ghassan Kanafani, called *A World Not Our Own*. It's a short story collection. The title caught my attention first, because it's exactly how I feel as a Palestinian – that I'm living in a world that is not mine. Because what world of mine would allow the killing of thousands of my countrymen and women? Or the forced displacement of the same population? The world is very big, yet I feel there is no space for me in it.

After each story, Ghassan writes the location that he was in and the year in which he wrote it. This makes me sad because I'm in Australia right now, writing about Gaza. I want to be in Gaza, writing about Gaza. I want to be able to sign my book, at the end, with 'Gaza 2023/2024', but I won't be able to. It's a small detail; perhaps I should focus on the bigger picture.

The first story in Ghassan's book describes a small boy who is gifted a goldfinch. He wonders why the bird keeps moving in its cage, until his older brother explains to him that birds need two to three months to adapt to new surroundings, and that he should expect the goldfinch to try to find a way to escape. Sympathizing, the little boy buys a bigger cage for the bird, hoping that the extra space will help it adapt faster. But it doesn't. The bird never adapts, and it dies anyway. It's not a happy story.

That goldfinch is every Palestinian. I find myself forcibly displaced to Australia, and I'm supposed to adapt. At least it's doable for somebody my age, but I keep thinking of teta. She's in her seventies, and she's been displaced so many times throughout her life. She's originally from Jaffa, but she managed to adapt to her life in Gaza, helped by the fact that she's excellent at socializing. But here in Australia? What's she supposed to do, start over in a new language at her age?

I feel rude writing this, but she's changed. She doesn't communicate with us any more. Her mind is completely and entirely in Gaza, so she stays hooked on the TV basically 24/7, waiting and watching for any news about home. She's lost in it. And she doesn't listen when I try to point it out.

In an interview, someone asks me what the Genocide has taught me. And I respond pretty aggressively, claiming that I knew a lot about life and that I didn't need a Genocide to teach me anything else. We eventually laugh about it, move on and that part of the interview never airs. But looking back on it, I think I was bitter because I hate the idea that I needed 33,000 (at last count) people to die in order to learn a lesson. It was a rude question to ask me.

I'm feeling happy today and I haven't felt that for so long that I'd almost forgotten what the word means.

Yara is here in Australia!

The last time I hung out with Yara was in Gaza on 6 October. I remember it like it was yesterday. It was a Friday, and the weather was nice and breezy. Yara and her dad came to pick me up from my house in her dad's silver Volkswagen Golf, and we went to a restaurant, Level Up – an iconic location, because of the views from its windows. It's one of the tallest buildings in Gaza; from it, you can see almost the entire Strip. It's ironic, and a bit sad, that I was there the day before the Genocide started.

When we arrived, the place was almost empty and we had our choice of where to sit. We sat at a table with a plug socket nearby, because we had our laptops and we were planning to apply for master's programmes together. We ordered two hot chocolates and a pizza – don't ask me how that combo works, it just does!

I've just realized that hot chocolate and pizza was the last proper meal I ever ate in Gaza.

We were talking about life after graduation, Yara and I, and about what the future would hold for us. I remember how we were both staring at the sky, telling each other how beautiful Gaza was, and how much potential She had were She not under occupation. We didn't actually apply to any universities that day – of course we didn't, we always talked more than we worked. Now, looking back at it, I'm grateful that we got to have that chat, and to say goodbye to Gaza together.

And then today, 6 April 2024, exactly six months since that lunch. Here we are, two girls from the Gaza Strip, an area that's only 365 square kilometres in total, hanging out in Melbourne, a city with an area of almost 10,000 square kilometres. I even text Yara before we go out, feeling nervous, as if it is my first time ever going out, and she says it is a mutual feeling. It's big!

We are texting about clothes, and she sends me a picture of her outfit, asking me if it is 'suitable'. She is wearing a basic black top! But she hasn't dressed up to go out since October last year, so she is anxious about it. That might seem like an unnecessary detail to you, but think about what state of mind she has to be in to think like that. I notice again how we Palestinians who experienced the Genocide have forgotten what normal life is supposed to be like.

Fast forward to when we met in the city. We spend the entire time talking about two things: one, Gaza, and our experiences over the last few months, and two, about how we should try to enjoy our time together and not talk about our trauma. Yes, of course, we fail on that second point. But you know what? It's always interesting for me to listen to people from Gaza talk about their feelings and experiences during the Genocide. It's crazy how every person experienced it in a different way.

Later on, we film a TikTok together. I love and enjoy filming TikToks, and when we do it together, I realize it is my first time doing one since October. And I feel *nervous.* About filming a TikTok. As if I was doing something new for the first time.

Never take things for granted, and enjoy every detail of your life. Your 'boring' day might be someone else's dream. I know that the above probably just sounds like a regular hangout to you, and you might think I'm making a lot out of nothing.

But there were days last year when I didn't think I'd make it out alive. And there have been days this year, in Australia, where I've felt safe but I didn't know if Yara would make it out alive, too. So if you'd told me six months ago that this is where we'd be, in Australia, safe and together, I don't think I would have believed you.

I had a conversation with Amin the other day about Palestinians, and our potential. Amin is Palestinian/Australian; he lives in Australia and we've become quite close friends with his family. I argued that we Palestinians are generally over-achievers because of our nationality. We're in a position where we have to put in twice as much effort just to make it in life, because being Palestinian means being seen as subhuman by the rest of the world. You always have to prove otherwise.

Then Amin mentioned Yara's dad, Maher, who immediately after arriving in Australia was brainstorming ideas about businesses he could start. At first, I didn't understand the point – to me, that seems normal. I'd even discussed business with Maher at the time. (I suggested he open a *manakeesh* restaurant, because he makes delicious *manakeesh* – especially those with zaatar.)

But Amin claimed that Maher's attitude was unusual. He said that he should rest, and it's sad that Palestinians feel that they constantly have to exist in survival mode, thinking of what's coming next all the time. And I was like – oh, he's actually right. I thought Maher's was a normal attitude to have, but for an *actually* normal person like Amin, who's Palestinian but grew up abroad, it was something that caught his attention. And now I agree with him and I can't unsee it. I just hate how Palestinians – at least those raised there – don't get the luxury of relaxing their minds even for a few hours when arriving in a new country.

On a positive note, something that I admire about us Palestinians is how creative we are. I actually like to call it a 'trauma glow-up', which means not living with a victim mentality, crying over what was – but instead, finding creative solutions to move forward. For example, the kids of Gaza. They no longer have toys to play with, but when I left they were using the electricity wires in the street as skipping ropes (no power, remember). Yes, we can cry for what we used to have; we're only humans, after all. But we don't stop there. We immediately get creative. Once, I saw a tent in Gaza built out of cans.

Now that's creativity.

You know what annoys me? Double standards. I genuinely do not understand people who support Palestine yet promote brands that are big on the boycott list.

Okay, so one thing about me is that I like to focus on positive behaviour, and support it where I see it. For example, I've never posted anything on social media about those who aren't boycotting; I've focused all my attention on those who are, supporting and thanking them. But this is my diary, so I'm safe to express my true feelings.

What annoys me the most is not even that they promote businesses that are on the boycott list. It's that they're posting about Palestine on their stories, rhetorically asking how they can help and saying they feel helpless, while they simultaneously profit from the brands that are supporting the destroyers of my homeland.

I'm not saying I'm perfect. I'm just a Palestinian girl trying her best to help her home in any way possible. When I was in Gaza, boycotting wasn't really an option, because access to basic necessities was limited. But now that I'm in Australia, I'm trying my best to boycott. A while ago, I bought shoes that were on sale and I didn't find out the brand was on the boycott list until two months later (Judy told me). It upset me, and since then, I've started to be more careful. I'm trying to live in a way that means I can sleep at night. If promoting a business that supports a Genocide allows someone to do that, then they can go ahead and do that. Nobody can force anyone into anything.

It's 4 a.m., by the way. I'm still awake because it's Ramadan, so I'm telling myself that makes it okay. I'm lying to myself, of course: my sleep schedule is so messed up, even if it wasn't Ramadan, I'd probably still be up.

#ABtalks just posted a podcast teaser trailer on Instagram and the episode features me. My friend Reem linked it to me and commented, reminding me how the interview show was one of the first things we had in common.

I'm emotional thinking about it, and her. I met Reem at Press House Palestine, back when it still existed. She participated in one of the workshops I ran for the English Media Club, and she was one of my favourites. She's a year younger than me, and we developed a strong bond over #ABtalks and everything else we had in common. We used to discuss our favourite episodes together constantly.

And now I've been on #ABtalks. I have a whole episode with Anas, the host, and it might become someone else's favourite episode, something that bonds two strangers like other episodes bonded me and Reem. I won't lie and claim I'm not happy about it.

But I just wish my appearance on the podcast had happened under different circumstances. And that I was back in Gaza, watching it with my friends and family.

It's time to get this out of my system and just write it down. I know it might sound selfish, but I'm tired of watching the news. Lately, I haven't been following it much. The only updates

I care about are those from my friends and cousins. I text them every day to make sure they're still alive. For now, that's all I need to know.

I don't even feel like writing any more. I'm just going to lie down, scroll through my phone and do absolutely nothing productive. Bye.

Yara and I go out again today. From the outside looking in, we seem like two normal tourists, nicely dressed and wandering around the city exploring. But inside, between us, we are just trying to feel something, talking about the Genocide the entire time we are together.

Yara says that, while she was displaced in a church, the IOF bombed part of it. And how after that, she started wearing her contact lenses while she slept. She tells me: 'What if the next time they bombed the building I was in, I got trapped under the rubble and I couldn't see anything?' I don't have much to say to this. I just listen. But the story will haunt me – she's one of my best friends.

On the train home, I see a lady with a suitcase, and the first thing that I think of is displacement, imagining how everyone in Gaza carries their whole life in their bag. What must be in this lady's suitcase? Important documents, surely? Maybe even an outfit? A cherished memory, if she was exceptionally lucky?

Then the announcement. 'Next stop: Malvern'. And I'm snapped back to my reality.

I'm in Australia now. I guess a suitcase can just be a suitcase.

I take the train again today. It's something I should do more often, because it's just so inspiring to have people around. When the train stops at Melbourne Central Station, almost half of the people in the carriage take off, and I start making up stories in my mind about what their various plans are for the day. The two girls sitting close to one another on the train – best friends off to grab coffee. The old man sitting next to me, reading a newspaper – he was on his way to a cafe, to reunite with an old friend.

It's funny how, only a couple of months ago, I was doing this in Gaza. I kept looking into people's eyes, trying to read their emotions. And the stories I'd imagine about them always revolved around whether they'd survive to the next day. I'd wonder about who was experiencing the last day of their lives in front of me.

It's different in Australia.

But that's enough – Yara is here, joining me in Brunetti. Bye for now.

After Gaza | MAY 2024

I usually tell you that the coming of a new month gives me hope. But today, it's not the fact that it's the beginning of May that's cheering me; it's the university students around the world, especially in the States. They are, I hope, changing the standards for us Palestinians.

See, we Palestinians have always harboured low expectations of the world, and we're always grateful for the bare minimum – which annoys me. But seeing students around the world today, speaking out, protesting and setting up encampments on their campuses, it's groundbreaking. It's beyond what I ever imagined.

Here's the thing: the students aren't just calling for a ceasefire. They're also calling for the establishment of the right of return, and insisting on a Palestine that is free from the River Jordan all the way to the Mediterranean Sea. They're advocating for a commercial and academic boycott of Israel. This is history.

Personally, my energy has been so drained the past couple of weeks, and I'm tired of interviews. However, no matter how busy or exhausted I am, I will never say no to talking to students and supporting them in any way. Interacting with students, and seeing how much my content resonates with children and young adults, is incredibly fulfilling. Growing up, I don't recall seeing journalists my age on TV, and I often felt disconnected from the news and the people reporting it. Now, the fact that this generation can learn about what's happening in Palestine from someone close to their age, someone they can relate to, brings me immense joy.

It's more than just reporting, though. It's about being a source of information *and* a role model for young people. They see that someone like them can be a voice for their community, can stand up and speak out on important issues. This connection not only educates them but also empowers them to believe in their own ability to make a difference. Knowing that I can contribute to shaping a more informed and engaged generation makes all the hard work worthwhile.

Every interaction with these young minds reinforces my commitment to my work. It's a reminder of why I started and why I must continue, despite the challenges I face. The energy and hope I see in their eyes give me the strength and motivation to keep pushing forward. Being Palestinian is a full-time job, but my occupation is more than just a job for me. It's a mission to inspire and educate the next generation of activists and changemakers.

I am bored today, so I ask mama if she would like to go out. She says yes; I call Yara, and we hatch a plan together for both of us and our mothers to go to the city in less than seven minutes. Efficiency!

We all meet and go to the State Library so our moms can see the building, then we go for dinner and a coffee (at Brunetti, of course). It is like a flashback to sixth grade, the last time the four of us all hung out together. That time had been at a restaurant called Lighthouse Gaza, and Yara and I had fought over something ridiculous at school. Back then, our moms brought us together so that we'd become friends; today, we were sitting there doing the same for them. Life is sometimes interesting and unpredictable.

While I'm enjoying lunch with my friend and her mom, the Genocide in Gaza is only getting worse. It's at the point that I feel the word Genocide is an understatement. The death toll is increasing faster than I thought it could. But I no longer have the energy or will to watch and follow the news, so today I didn't watch any. I just check to see if my relatives and friends in Gaza are alive. So far, they are.

I am devastated, and I go to speak to Khalo Khaled about how annoying it is to live in a world where you're treated like an object, and where you can see how everyone around you is just using your trauma for their marketing purposes.

I won an award last month from a group abroad. From the outset, I made clear to the organizers that I wouldn't be able to travel there, because I'm in the process of renewing my passport and I'm on a single-entry visa to Australia. (Also, if that wasn't enough, the country the group is based in doesn't grant visas to Palestinians from Gaza.) They responded that they had to limit the winners to those who would 'want' to attend the ceremony personally. Funny how they still claimed they wanted to honour my leadership and contribution. The point of the story isn't the award. It's about how, months into a Genocide, people will use someone's trauma to market themselves – and how they can be so disrespectful that they'll only agree to use you when it suits *them*.

I'm so put off by people or organizations that sell their values. The Genocide has been such an eye-opening experience. The current version of me – Genocide Plestia – is receiving opportunities and chances that the pre-Genocide version of me could have only dreamed of. But I don't see them the same way as I did before. I have to be careful, because I only want to work with people or organizations that interact with me for who I really am, not for how many followers I have.

Khalo Khaled always gives the best advice. I love him so much, he's always one of the first people I turn to. He tells me that the real joy of life lies in the journey, not the arrival, and I do agree with that. But he also tells me the Jim Carrey quote: 'I think everybody should get rich and famous and do everything they ever dreamed of so they can see it's not the answer.' If I'd heard that before I was famous, I would have laughed and dismissed it as something rich people say. But now I see the truth in it, and I second it: fame isn't the answer.

I can't deny that my fame has given me access to an endless number of opportunities that I wouldn't have gotten if I wasn't so well known. But what's the point in everything if, at the end of the day, you don't feel happy or at peace?

Earlier today, I was scrolling through Instagram. My feed is usually filled with images and videos of dead bodies, cries for hope and endless displacement. But suddenly I came across a picture of someone I follow, just sitting in a cafe drinking coffee. It startled me, and made me pause, realizing just how desensitized I've become to images of destruction and death. Now, what catches my attention is a glimpse of normal life.

We live in a sad world. That's all for today. I go to lie in my bed, to share my thoughts with the ceiling above me as I wait to fall asleep.

All I feel is emptiness. I don't remember the last time I felt this empty. I feel like I'm standing in the ashes of whoever I used to be. Whenever someone asks me questions about myself, I don't have answers. I feel like I don't know myself any more.

I answer with old answers that are no longer true. I keep saying that my favourite colour is yellow but is it? It *was* yellow. I used to have a lot of yellow shirts and shoes, but now I don't have any. No yellow items in my closet. Yellow is a happy colour, and my mental state is far from happy, so I can't lie to myself and wear yellow.

Whenever someone asks me about my favourite movie, I say *The Perks of Being a Wallflower*. But that was ages ago. The last time I watched it I was seventeen years old and I hadn't lived through a Genocide. Now I'm twenty-two, and I don't think I'd enjoy it if I watched it again.

My hobbies used to be reading and writing, but now whenever I read, I find it hard to focus. I started reading that book by Ghassan Kanafani, but it was so relatable that it made me feel more depressed, so I stopped. Then I googled 'interesting novels', but every time I tried to read one, I felt delusional and guilty reading a novel that has nothing to do with what's happening back home. As if there are other worlds out there that should continue while mine crumbles.

Who am I? Other than a displaced Palestinian journalist, who the world expects to be the perfect victim; who am I, really? I want to look in the mirror and be able to recognize the person staring back at me. I don't want to feel like I'm a body without a soul.

Maybe tomorrow, I will.

I've often asked myself,
If you went back to 6 October, how would you spend your time?
I wish I had hung out with Shima, just for an hour,
Chatting about life, and the books she's been reading.
A car ride with Haya, saying goodbye to the streets,
To the buildings, the places, all etched in my heart.

Then lunch at Bellini, seeing Ali's warm smile,
Greeting each customer, his joy in the air.
For the rest of the day? Sitting on the peach couch at home,
Watching TV with Dana, feeling the innocence of comfort and peace.
These moments I cherish are now dreams of the past.
If only I'd known, I'd have held them so tight.
In my heart, they remain, a bittersweet memory,
Of a day I'd relive, if I only had the chance.

It's insane to me how I lived through so many 'last times' in Gaza without being aware of it. There was a last time I walked Gaza's streets. There was a last time I worked at Press House Palestine. There was a last time hanging out with Dana on a Thursday. There was a last time swimming in Gaza's sea, a last time sleeping comfortably in my own room, a last time standing in front of my closet and complaining about having nothing to wear. And there was a last time I was a version of myself that I knew.

There have been times when I've felt forced to appear grateful that I survived and made it out alive, when deep down I didn't feel grateful at all. I've felt what it is to be a Palestinian from Gaza in the eyes of the world, dehumanized to the point that being alive is something to be thankful for, because you didn't end up killed like the rest.

I can't deny that there are things that I'm grateful for. I didn't want to lose parts of my body. I'm physically okay. But am I grateful that I was able to leave Gaza while others stay there facing the Israeli Genocide? Am I grateful that my chance to show the world my home, through my eyes, came at the cost of my family being constantly terrified for my life? Am I grateful that some people get to survive, and others don't, and that the killings are completely indiscriminate and random? No, I'm not – not for any of it. And that's okay. I've learned that it's okay not to feel grateful for everything. This is my experience, after all.

What scares me the most is waking up without any emotion. For a while now, I haven't really felt anything. I'm not sad. I'm not happy. I don't even feel numb. I just wake up and exist every day.

Today I woke up feeling angry and, for that, I am grateful.

Today is 15 May 2024. Today marks the seventy-sixth anniversary of Al-Nakba in 1948, which I think we have to say is still ongoing. It never really ended, did it? My grandparents shared stories with me about Al-Nakba, and one day I'll share with my grandchildren stories about a continuous Nakba in 2023 and 2024. I hope that the cycle stops with me, and that my grandkids go on to share with their world the story of a Free Palestine.

Today is the El-Kurd twins' birthday. Mohammed and Mona are two Palestinian activists known for the Save Sheikh Jarrah movement. I remember that today is their birthday because it falls on Nakba Day. Similarly, I know Samah Sabawi's birth year because it coincides with Al-Naksa, when thousands of Palestinians were displaced from their homes in 1967. I wish Palestinian birthdays didn't revolve around tragedies but they do. Remember how my birthday is on Human Rights Day? It's funny, I know. You can laugh.

I long for the day when a child will feel unique joy because their birthday coincides with the anniversary of a Free Palestine. It's the only vision that keeps my spirit alive.

Irony follows me everywhere. When I was reporting from Gaza, I felt that there were lots of restrictions on what I could post. I always chose my words and posts carefully, fearing that what I said might trigger Israel to target me or my family. Naively, I thought that once I left Gaza, I'd be free to post or share whatever I wanted. That's not the case.* I've come to learn that language can be weaponized anywhere. The only difference is that, in Gaza, we're not allowed to protect ourselves from the potential attack.

During my time in Gaza, I never fully understood what I was going through because everyone around me was living the same tragedy. Now, here in Australia, thousands of kilometres away from home, everything is different. Yet I wake up every day not understanding how I ended up here, and I ask myself, is this my life now? One day, I was safe at home, and the next day I was displaced in Al-Quds Hospital, then Amal's house, then Rasha's house, then at my uncles' house in Khan Younis – and now to a different continent, no longer even in Gaza at all. My brain still can't comprehend it.

Like, now what? How is one supposed to process everything I've witnessed? How is one supposed to believe in human rights? How is one supposed to live and love life again, after becoming so starkly aware of the true nature of the world we're living in? There are too many questions going around my head, and I don't know how I'm supposed to answer them.

* This book has been read by teams of lawyers in multiple different countries.

For the longest time, I felt survivor's guilt. But recently, I realized that I'm only a small part of it. We're all puppets in the same production. The reality is that we cannot change the world, not as a primary action: instead, we have to try not to let the world change our hearts, and try to find hope through that.

The only thing keeping me sane right now is witnessing the world finally starting to wake up, to recognize our humanity, our love and our unbreakable faith. I'm grateful that I've lived to see the day when I can proudly say that I'm from Palestine, and people not only recognize it but understand its significance. The world has seen the incredible strength of our people and the boundless depth of our hope.

Golda Meir, the fourth prime minister of Israel, once justified her nation's atrocities by reassuring her people that the old would die, and the young would forget. But that hasn't happened. My generation has proven to the world that while the old may die, the young will not forget, ensuring that our collective memories and dreams will never fade.

Every night, amidst the chaos and despair, I hold on to the belief that Palestine will one day be free. And on that day, birthdays will be celebrated – not just for life, but for the freedom we fought so desperately hard to achieve.

I knew Gaza before 7 October 2023. I've known Gaza throughout the Genocide. But I have yet to know the Gaza of tomorrow.

I knew the version of myself before 7 October 2023, and I've known myself throughout the Genocide. But I have yet to meet the Plestia that survived.

I am only sure of one thing, and that's that no matter where life takes me, and no matter what happens to my beloved Gaza, we will always be part of each other.

Ceasefire

Wars do not end when the bombs stop falling.

Ceasefire | SUNDAY 19 JANUARY

How can you unlive everything you've lived? How can you unhear everything you've heard? How can you unsee everything you've witnessed?

I am overwhelmed with emotions. I don't think there is a word to describe how you feel after more than fourteen months of a Genocide.

The first thing I did when I heard the news of a ceasefire was call Dana. The minute I heard her voice, I started tearing up. I allowed myself to cry all the uncried tears that I've been keeping inside me for the past year and a half. My biggest fear was Dana getting killed. Tonight, for the first time, I can sleep knowing that Dana – and all my other beloved ones in Gaza – will be alive tomorrow.

But I can't stop myself from thinking: why is the Palestinian always the exception to everything – exempt from the world's recognition of suffering and exempt from the right to joy? Happiness after a war ends, gratefulness when a Palestinian hostage is set free, and joy when electricity briefly returns – these are emotions that only Palestinians seem to understand. These moments highlight the grim reality that even emotions, natural human reactions, are a privilege not afforded to all.

I think of the orphans. I think of those who have lost loved ones. I think of all Palestinians. For them, do wars ever really end? A ceasefire might stop the missiles, but the trauma remains.

This ceasefire is not an end; it's a pause. Wars do not end when the bombs stop falling. They linger in the minds of those who survive and in the void left by those who do not. For Palestinians, the war is never over – ceasefire is merely the space between tragedies. And in that space, we carry with us the unbearable weight of memories that cannot be undone.

What is Home?

What is Home?
Growing up I thought,
Home is a four-walled house,
Where my mom bakes my favourite cake,
My dad works on the balcony,
My brother watches TV on the couch,
And my sister annoys my brother,

But the four-walled house was bombed.
Do homes get bombed? No.

Maybe home is the people I love.
But the people I love were killed.
Do homes get killed? No.

Then home is surely Gaza.
The place where I was born,
The place where I experienced all my firsts.
But Gaza was erased.
Do homes get erased? No.

Plestia Alaqad

If houses were bombed,
People were killed,
And Gaza was erased,
Then please tell me
What is home?
Where can I find it?

Home is the sea,
Vast and enduring,
Its waves carefree.

No bomb can shatter it,
No force can kill it,
No erasure can diminish it.

Home is the sea,
And no one can change that.

The story doesn't end here.
The story is yet to start.
May we live to narrate it.

Through all this
The question remains
How do you get over a Genocide?

The End

How do you get over a Genocide?

Acknowledgements

First and foremost, always and forever, I thank God. Making it out alive was a miracle that I often underestimate.

I remember the first day of university when I went to the wrong class, and the professor gave us a piece of advice that stayed with me: be careful who you make friends with, because you become who you surround yourself with. Ever since then, I've always been selective with who I spend time around.

With that being said, I want to give a special thank you to everyone I've ever crossed paths with: you are part of who I am today.

To the strangers that I met in Gaza, who became my family: thank you for trusting me with your stories. And to my online family, who waited for my diary entries to make sure I was still alive: thank you for seeing me for who I am, not just as a number or a statistic or a headline.

To my literary agent, Kemi, who has represented *The Eyes of Gaza* in the best way possible: thank you for making publishing my first book a smooth experience. To my editor, Ause Abdelhaq, who had to keep up with all my stubbornness: lol, I owe you one. And to everyone else who touched this book – copy-editors, designers, lawyers and fact-checkers – thank you for helping me bring it to life.

To Rupi Kaur: thank you for offering your constant guidance. You are like the older sister I never had. To the sister I do have, Judy, who gave me her phone to work and report from even when it was the last thing she wanted to do: without you, I would've been a boring and bored person, stuck in the corner of a tent with no way to share my thoughts with the world. And to my other sister, Yara Tarazi, who listened to all my traumatic stories: together, without even realizing it, we healed something in each other.

To Auntie Samah Sabawi, Amo Amin Abbas and Amo Maher Mughrabi: thank you for being the first people to read the manuscript and offer me feedback. Your wisdom, advice and support have meant the world.

To Khalo Tareq, who saved my family and I: you initially annoyed me, because I didn't want to be saved – but now, I am thankful.

To Khalo Khaled: thank you for being the best uncle and mentor. Your endless patience, guidance and advice has made me a better version of myself.

To my dad: thank you for giving me the space to be the person I am today. To my brother: thank you for being the calm sibling, so I can be the wild one. To my entire family: I couldn't have anything without you. And to my close friends: thank you for loving and accepting all versions of Plestia.

Last but not least, to mama and teta Fatma, my second mom. This book would have not been possible without you. No thank you will ever be enough.

And to all the generations yet to come – may you read this book in a free Palestine.

Dear reader,

Thank you for reaching the end of this book. Sharing my diary felt like baring my soul – raw, vulnerable, and exposing. Yet what gave me the courage to do so is knowing that people like you are out there – people who genuinely care, who stand with Palestine and who remind me that our stories matter.

I hope this book left you feeling something, whether it was anger, sorrow, hope or a mix of it all. Because to feel is to be alive, and as long as we're alive, we can fight. We can fight for a world where no child grows up hearing the hum of drones instead of lullabies, where no family fears being torn apart by forces beyond their control, and where no one goes to sleep dreading the loss of their body, their home or their dreams.

We are all stories. Everyone in Gaza is a story. And you, too, have a story. Let it be one worth living, one worth remembering. Use your story to make the world better, kinder and more just.

Thank you for listening to mine.

With unwavering hope,
Plestia Alaqad